Praise for *The Paradox of Excellence*

"Extremely clear and concise with actual remedies instead of only theories. A must-read for anyone with sales, marketing, and general management responsibilities."

> —Jackie Meyer, marketing director,
> Qualcomm Wireless Business Solutions

"David Mosby and Michael Weissman have hit the nail on the head with this interesting and understandable look at how outstanding performance can ultimately shipwreck a healthy organization."

> —Tim Allen, senior director of operations,
> Ingram Micro Logistics

"You put words to my intuition. I have been struggling with this issue and now it has a name! *The Paradox of Excellence* is a must-read for start-ups, mature companies, and service providers alike. Our company has already begun shattering the paradox and continuing our pursuit of excellence."

> —Pierce Plam, CEO, Dealer Fusion, Inc.

"This book should be required reading of every sales team—without exception! In this day of hyper competition, the seemingly simple task of reminding our customers about our value and the impact we've had on their businesses should be paramount. Forgetting this simple rule of thumb could result in the loss of so many things both valuable and important to us: our customer relationships, our market share, and our strong reputation amongst our peers."

—Marc Mandel, global strategic solutions manager, OneSource Information Services Inc.

"*The Paradox of Excellence* does an excellent job of describing one of the overlooked subtleties of selling and managing client relationships."

—Bill Nichols, managing director, Milpitas Dedicated Fulfillment Center, Comac, an Iron Mountain Company

"Hidden in *The Paradox of Excellence* is a big idea: that expectations and satisfaction are dynamic and interdependent. As a market researcher, that idea has big implications. Yet, as a student of human nature, I am now convinced the idea's impact could be even bigger. This little tome could influence how families, employees, companies, and other groups interact—for the good!"

—Michael Kelly, CEO, Techtel Corporation

"*The Paradox of Excellence* is something all organizations should be aware of. It is simply not enough to be excellent if one allows customers or competitors to define the playing field. Mosby and Weissman point out beautifully that organizations such as these need to constantly provide the context for which they want to be judged."

—Brian Barefoot, president, Babson College, and former senior managing director, Merrill Lynch

"Any company's pursuit of excellence is not without its unintended consequences. Mosby and Weissman have done a masterful job in raising awareness and preparing business leaders to create a profitable and sustainable competitive advantage. If you have an 'ear to hear' the message of *The Paradox of Excellence,* it's a must-read."

—Len DiGiovanni, president, Impact, Inc.

"This book describes perfectly how we fall victim to *The Paradox of Excellence.* We have a saying in our office: 'you're only as good as your last mistake.' The creative services industry is very different from the shipping company described in the book. However, the problem is identical to the ones we face with our long-term clients. I will use what I've learned in this book to ensure we don't turn some of our minor mistakes into crises."

—Patty Jensen, vice president, client services, Jensen Design Associates

"In today's fast-paced environment, it is easy to neglect the aspects of life that are not troublesome. *The Paradox of Excellence* reminds us of the importance of the aspects of life that work or operate well. It provides another tool to eliminate poor communication as a reason to have problems."

—Bob Verret, CIO, Integres Global Logistics

"The lessons learned in *The Paradox of Excellence* apply not only to companies of all sizes but to individual professionals like myself as well. As a realtor, client referrals are the way I grow my business, and this book has taught me how to keep my superb performance on the minds of my clients."

> —John A. Brassner, realtor, Coldwell Banker Premier Realty, Las Vegas

"Ostensibly a business book essential to managers, but under the covers it's filled with insight for everyone in the enterprise. Taking you through a quick succession of alternately entertaining and thought-provoking chapters, it gave me a new perspective on communicating our company's strengths. As a must-read for the whole team, *The Paradox of Excellence* has also helped us shape our product to reach out to our customers in new ways. Bravo!"

> —Sam M. Sawires, CEO, Salveo, Inc.

"Talk about a book that applies to all businesses! I was a bit skeptical when I first picked up the book, thinking that *The Paradox of Excellence* probably wouldn't apply to my business—architecture. But wow was I wrong. In the course of the following hour, I discovered that yes, we suffer from the same issues. I see now that we need to constantly reinforce our excellent performance with our clients—not just when we market a new client or compete for a specific design opportunity—but continually while we provide services. We have known for years the value of repeat clients, and generally we have been successful. But with this new understanding, there is no reason why we can't sustain our client relationships for years to come."

—Bob Riegel, principal, The KPA Group,
Oakland/San Francisco, California

"There are no simple, smooth transactions in the real estate business. Difficulties always occur. To provide stress-free transactions for clients, real estate professionals usually try to give the appearance of a smooth process when dealing with clients. Since reading *The Paradox of Excellence*, I have been experimenting with being more frank with clients— discussing the difficulties and how I've resolved them. As a result, I have found client satisfaction with my service has gone way, way up! I'd highly recommend this book to anyone who provides any kind of service to others."

—Paul Grabowsky, mortgage broker,
Coast to Coast Funding

"Anyone running a services or specialty retail business should take *The Paradox of Excellence* to heart. Mosby and Weissman illustrate the importance of understanding your business through the customer's eyes and reinforce the real costs of failing to match your service with their perception of value. As founder of a company involved in helping customers reach their goals for fitness and wellness, I found *The Paradox of Excellence* very useful in creating customer retention and renewal programs."

—Steve Bertges, founder, Fit to GO Studios, Inc.

"*The Paradox of Excellence* is a great 'new' frame of reference that people can easily latch on to. It was a pleasure to read."

—Jon Safer, president, Bridge International
Group, LLC

"The parable made it possible and even fun to read for me. Any organization that is trying to better itself and its image could use this info."

—Joan Wright, career public school teacher (retired)

"*The Paradox of Excellence* has put everyday work problems into something every profession can use. Even in health care, where patient care is our 'product,' the paradox of excellence rings true when your customer is used to getting the very best care, and only says something when a problem arises. The book reminds us that nothing is perfect, and by getting our patients' expectations under control we can then provide to them some concrete evidence of our value to their process of rehabilitation."

—Julie Choate, MPT, Physiotherapy Associates

"I enjoyed reading *The Paradox of Excellence* and saw many parallels in our wireless infrastructure business. We provide an invisible commodity to the end consumer, unless there's an outage. After reading the book, we have started to build new systems that make our true performance more visible to customers."

—Clark Smith, president, Western States
    Teleport

"We always see the difficult, rarely the obvious. After reading *The Paradox of Excellence,* I am now more aware of how the paradox affects every area of our lives."

—Jeff Eitzen, pastor of worship and arts,
    Creekside Community Church

THE

OF
EXCELLENCE

How
Great Performance
Can *Kill* Your
Business

DAVID MOSBY and
MICHAEL WEISSMAN

JOSSEY-BASS
A Wiley Imprint
www.josseybass.com

Published by Jossey-Bass
A Wiley Imprint
989 Market Street, San Francisco, CA 94103-1741
www.josseybass.com

Jossey-Bass books and products are available through most bookstores. To contact Jossey-Bass directly call our Customer Care Department within the U.S. at 800-956-7739, outside the U.S. at 317-572-3986, or fax 317-572-4002.

Jossey-Bass also publishes its books in a variety of electronic formats. Some content that appears in print may not be available in electronic books.

Library of Congress Cataloging-in-Publication Data

Mosby, David, 1948-
    The paradox of excellence : how great performance can kill your business / by David Mosby and Michael Weissman.
        p. cm.
    ISBN-13 978-0-7879-8139-6 (alk. paper)
    ISBN-10 0-7879-8139-7 (alk. paper)
    1. Success in business.   2. Management.   3. Customer relations.   I. Weissman, Michael, 1965-   II. Title.
    HF5386.M79 2005
    658.8'12—dc22   2005013190

Printed in the United States of America
FIRST EDITION
HB Printing   10 9 8 7 6 5 4 3 2 1

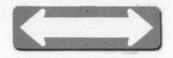

Contents

PART TWO: The Models

Introduction

The famous physicist Albert Einstein reportedly once said, "Try not to become a man of success but rather a man of value." It's great advice, and we've met thousands of people struggling to become people of value. Yet as these people strive for excellence, their efforts are increasingly taken for granted, and their excellent performance is often devalued. You might feel the same way.

Organizations are also frequently undervalued. Since the 1980s, many organizations have implemented continuous improvement and customer intimacy initiatives in a quest for sustained market leadership and lasting value. But customer loyalty has plunged to all-time lows, and shareholder value has become more volatile than at any other time in history. Companies that have successfully implemented these improvement initiatives are not getting the expected value from them, but instead are becoming more invisible because of them. It's a phenomenon that we identify in the book title and throughout: *The Paradox of Excellence.*

The paradox of excellence is that the better you do your job, the more your performance becomes invisible. Improved performance does not necessarily translate into higher perceived value. In fact, it is more likely to shift the customer's view of commodity performance upward and cause the customer to take that new, improved performance for granted. Vendors that perform extraordinarily well set a customer expectation for themselves that is often difficult to sustain.

Part One of *The Paradox of Excellence* is a management story that illustrates the symptoms and causes of the paradox and provides a clear way to overcome it. The story highlights what happens when a vendor allows a single negative situation to characterize and define an entire relationship between itself and its customer.

We have tried to create an entertaining story with characters you can relate to, ideas you can use, and practical frameworks to help you achieve the long-term success you desire. While the characters and organizations are all fictitious, they represent composites of real people in real organizations with whom we've worked. Just like all of us, they exhibit courage and fear, strength and weakness, humility and arrogance, altruism and greed, all in varying degrees. They laugh, panic, cheer, stumble, delight, sink, and fly with hope. And just like them, we have daily opportunities to find ways to prevail over the hidden obstacles we all face.

Part Two contains three sections: "The Concept," an overview of the paradox of excellence; "The Assessment," a twenty-question self-assessment you can use to determine your vulnerability to the paradox; and "The Roadmap for Success," a series of steps you can follow to quickly and easily overcome the paradox of excellence.

We know you're busy, so we wrote this book to be read in one or two sittings. We've chosen the parable format because stories are better remembered than formulas, plus they're far more fun to read (and to write)! We encourage you to read *The Paradox of Excellence* with an open heart and an open mind, and we hope this book will both entertain you and help you develop sustained value in all areas of your life.

PART ONE: The Story

The Crisis

"How Could This Happen?"

The Way Out

Victory

The Interviews

The Crisis

Chapter 1

It was 9:20 A.M. Monday morning, and Tom Fredericks was already having a very bad day. Just a few weeks ago he had joined Premiere Specialty Trucking, a mid-sized logistics company servicing California's Silicon Valley, as their new sales and marketing VP, and now a major account was disappearing before his eyes. Tom reread the "Termination of Services" e-mail from MacroZip Electronics, Premiere's largest and most prestigious customer. *What just happened?* he wondered to himself.

"Ryan, get in here!" Tom yelled to the account rep handling MacroZip, who was sitting in the sales bullpen outside his door.

Ryan Walters grabbed some paper and hustled into Tom's office. Ryan had never before heard Fredericks raise his voice. "What's up, boss?"

"This." Tom pushed the e-mail toward Ryan.

Ryan's face paled as he read the word TERMINATION in the curtly written e-mail from Gary Howard, vice president of logistics for MacroZip Electronics. "They're firing us? This is unbelievable! I've worked with MacroZip for over five years, and there's been no sign that anything was wrong."

"Well, I think it's fair to say we *now* have a pretty good sign something's horribly wrong! Go find out what the heck's going on and get me a meeting with Gary Howard while I go get chewed out by Peters." Tom was referring to his boss, Hank Peters, the tough-minded, no-nonsense founder and CEO of Premiere Trucking. Tom fumed while he walked toward his boss's office.

Hank Peters sat on the edge of his gray metal desk with a phone to his ear, barking instructions to a dispatcher. The sixty-year-old retired Marine master sergeant was a force of nature. His military record had shown him to be gifted at sorting out and successfully arranging complex puzzle pieces of logistics, politics, and positioning to ensure the survival of his troops. In the twenty years since his retirement from the Corps, he had built one of the best-run shipping companies in the country and clearly the best in his local market. In both careers he lived by the motto "Excellence Delivers Victory!"

"Hold on," Peters said, cupping his phone. "What?" he growled, as Tom's head popped through the door. One didn't barge in on Hank Peters. He preferred structure, organization, and discipline. If you wanted to see him, you'd better have an appointment.

"Mr. Peters, sorry to interrupt. We have a crisis, and I need to talk to you," Tom replied.

"Can it wait?"

"No sir. I don't think it can."

"Okay. Stan, I'll have to call you back." Peters hung up the phone. "Now, just what's so important that it can't wait until our 11:00 management meeting?"

"This," Tom said, swallowing hard and handing the e-mail to Peters.

Peters put on his reading glasses and quickly scanned the email. "Tom," he said sternly, looking above his glasses, "MacroZip Electronics has been my client for over a dozen years. I personally sold and managed them. You haven't even been here a month. Explain to me how you managed to lose our largest customer!"

"Mr. Peters, I don't know what prompted this e-mail. It just came in. I've asked Ryan, who handles MacroZip, to provide me with some answers. I'll try to get you an explanation by our 11 A.M. meeting, but I wanted you to know about this as soon as possible," Tom replied.

"Trying won't cut it. I want answers. Get it done!" Peters shouted, picking up the phone and dismissing Tom with a wave of his hand.

Chapter 2

"Ryan!" Tom shouted when he returned to his office. "What's the situation with MacroZip?"

"I called their warehouse manager. He told me we messed up MacroZip's shipment to Single, the hot-selling mobile gaming device company, which was due on Friday. The shipment didn't show up until this morning," Ryan said, shuffling into Tom's office.

"Why? What the hell happened?"

"I don't know exactly. I'm trying to find out. I can't find the dispatcher in charge, so I haven't tracked down who handled the shipment yet."

"Well, stay on it," Tom said. "What else did the warehouse manager say?"

"The guys at MacroZip are really ticked off. They trusted us. MacroZip was already in trouble with Single. Apparently, another trucking company had frequently delivered late to Single. To fix that problem, MacroZip moved the bulk of their local trucking business to us. Until this weekend, we'd eliminated the late-delivery problem. But because we hadn't delivered the parts until this morning, Single had to shut down their factory on Sunday. It was the final straw for Single. They notified MacroZip of their intent to find another supplier of electronic parts, and MacroZip is blaming us for everything. From MacroZip's perspective, we blew it when they had needed us to come through the most. They feel like we lied to them—like we misled them. Now they don't know why they ever trusted us."

"Did we mislead them?"

"No . . . not intentionally . . ." Ryan stammered, trying to find the right words. "Quality is how we've distinguished ourselves from the competition, right? It's how we won all that business at MacroZip in the first place. Our mantra has always been "Excellence Delivers Victory!" You know—Hank's thing. It's right there on your wall." Ryan pointed to the motivational picture hanging behind Tom's chair with those very words. "Everything we communicate to our customers drives home that point. So did we mislead them? No. Our performance has been great—at least up 'til now. Going forward, though, we may have to mislead people."

"Why?"

"How am I supposed to talk with our customers given what's happened? If excellence delivers victory, what do screw-ups deliver?"

"I hear ya," Tom winced, and then quickly turned serious. "But Ryan, we need to fix this situation right now. Your job is on the line, and so is mine. When am I scheduled to meet with Gary Howard?"

"I've set up a call between you and Gary at 2:00 today. He's stuck in a meeting until then."

"Fine. In the meantime, go buy the MacroZip warehouse manager some lunch. Try mending the fence as best you can."

"Consider it done," Ryan said, as he walked out of Tom's office.

Chapter 3

Twenty minutes later, Tom popped two Advil to ward off the colossal headache clawing its way into his brain. He had just gotten off the phone with his wife, Trish, relating his conversations with Peters and Ryan and longing for an encouraging word. He wasn't sure he'd have a job by the end of the day, given how things were proceeding.

Unfortunately, the phone call had only raised the stakes, which were already very high. The Fredericks had just bought an expensive home on a hill overlooking the city, and the fear of losing the house had sent his wife into a panic-stricken barrage of questions: "What will we do? Will we have to move again? What about the kids? Will they have to switch schools? They've finally made some friends. Would Jumbo Logistics take you back?" It was not the kind of talk he needed right now.

I probably should have done more due diligence before coming to Premiere, he thought while assembling his notes in preparation for his management meeting. Yet everyone had said Premiere was the best place to work. While Old Man Peters had been cocky to name the company Premiere in the beginning, the company had lived up to the billing. It had acquired a great reputation as a just-in-time logistics services company where precise delivery is paramount. It was the reason Tom had joined the company in the first place. Before joining Premiere, he had rapidly reached the level of regional sales manager at Jumbo Logistics, a larger national firm. At thirty-four years of age, this was his first opportunity to be a vice president, and he thought Premiere was the best place in the industry to work. That is, up until today.

Tom looked up at the clock: 10:55 A.M. He stood up, collected his hastily assembled notes, and headed off to the weekly management meeting—the standard forum for the management team to report on every aspect of Premiere's business. Of all the meetings in his life, he was not going to be late for this one.

Carolyn Arnold, VP of operations, took the seat, as always, next to Hank Peters. A smart, outspoken woman in her late forties, Carolyn was as tough as Peters. She had been at Premiere almost since the beginning. It was her life. Next to Peters, she was the most senior person on the management team and was actively seeking the CEO job upon Peters' retirement. Next to Carolyn sat Anne Simpson, the company's financial manager. A former public accountant, Anne oversaw all information systems, company finances, and HR matters. Both women had earned Peters' confidence, something Tom had yet to achieve, and he wasn't going to be helped by today's news.

At exactly 11 A.M., Peters started the meeting. "Okay, people. I'm tossing out our normal agenda. We have a crisis, and it's going to drive our discussion this morning. Tom, tell them the situation," Peters gestured toward the other executives.

Tom cleared his throat and sipped some coffee, praying he would sound more confident than he felt. As the youngest member of the management team, his peers looked at him with some skepticism. "This morning, MacroZip Electronics gave us notice of termination."

A chorus of disbelief and protest broke out among the other executives when they heard this earth-shattering news. The loss of MacroZip would wipe away their yearly bonuses. The company would lose over 20 percent of its revenue, and that would mean layoffs. Premiere didn't have fat. Good, hardworking people would definitely lose their jobs.

"Keep it down, folks." Peters cut off the conversation with a swipe of his hand. "Tom, tell us what you've learned since we talked this morning."

"Thank you, sir. On Friday, we misplaced a shipment of MacroZip Electronics parts destined for Single. As a result, Single couldn't manufacture products yesterday. Single is apparently terminating their relationship with MacroZip, and MacroZip is definitely terminating their relationship with us. From what

I've learned, it was an operations quality issue on our part."

As he spoke, Tom looked over uncomfortably at Carolyn Arnold. Tom hadn't wanted to go head-to-head with her. He knew how much Peters relied on her and trusted her. However, he honestly did believe it was her department's fault, and the recent conversation with his wife had bolstered his need to protect his turf.

Carolyn looked right through Tom as if he didn't exist. She didn't agree with Tom's hire but had acquiesced when Peters picked Tom over her candidate. Carolyn would have to keep Tom in check if she wanted to secure the CEO slot. Any more attacks like this one and Tom wouldn't last long in her regime. *I wonder if Tom knows that Peters is thinking about retiring,* she thought to herself.

"Carolyn," Peters said. "Go get me some facts. I'm trying to set up a call with my old buddy, Frank

Sommers, who's now the COO* at MacroZip. He's out of the office until late tomorrow. Therefore, I want us to meet at 8 A.M. tomorrow, and I'd better have some answers from all of you on what the heck happened and how we get out of this situation. I will *NOT* lose this client. Are we clear?" Peters looked around the room, meeting everyone's eyes with a hard stare to accentuate the point and guarantee agreement.

"The rest of you, we're done. Tom, stay behind for a moment," Peters said, ending the meeting.

Damn. This is it, Tom thought, bracing himself for the firing he felt was unjustified but nonetheless coming.

Peters walked over to Tom, who was still sitting. With his piercing blue eyes Hank Peters said, "Tom, I hired you because I believed in you. Now go prove I made a wise decision." With that, he turned around and walked out the door.

---

* Chief operating officer

Chapter 4

Carolyn Arnold was fuming. She ran the tightest ship in the industry. "Excellence Delivers Victory!" was her mantra as well, and she had delivered that excellence virtually every day. The CEO brass ring was rightfully hers. There was no way some kid still wet behind the ears was going to mess it up for her.

She quickly assembled her team to brief them on what had happened in the meeting and began to put the pieces together. Unfortunately, she discovered that Tom was, in fact, correct. Operations had blown it on Friday. There had been a mix-up.

Part of a shipment destined for Single's San Jose plant had never made it onto the right truck. Premiere was handling two shipments for MacroZip on Friday: one destined for San Diego and another destined for San Jose. An important pallet of electronic parts earmarked for San Jose had accidentally been combined with the shipment destined for the gaming company's operation in San Diego. All hell broke loose at Single late Friday when the San Jose delivery was unloaded and the parts weren't there. By the time they traced the problem back to Premiere, the missing parts were three hundred miles away on the Premiere truck in Southern California.

Premiere made every attempt to get the product back to Single's San Jose factory in time. The driver and dispatcher coordinated with Single's receiving department and explained the situation. They all agreed that if Premiere could get the product to San Jose by noon on Saturday, everything would be fine. Noon was a firm deadline, because Single's dock-workers were forbidden to work late on Saturdays. The receiving dock would be closed until Monday morning. Premiere's driver agreed to drive all the way through the night to make it back.

Sometimes, however, the best-laid plans succumb to the evils of fate. On the truck's drive back from Southern California early Saturday morning, a fatal accident shut down the freeway for hours. The resulting traffic snarl cost the driver the better part of a day. Premiere's dispatchers tried myriad ways to remedy the situation, but there was no possible way to get the parts to Single on time. By the time the exhausted driver arrived at Single's San Jose warehouse late Saturday afternoon, the crew had already gone home. Consequently, Premiere's truck couldn't deliver the goods until 8:00 Monday morning—and by that time it was too late. It was a "perfect storm" of circumstances.

Our service to MacroZip has been near perfect for a really long time, Carolyn thought. *They can't be leaving us over this one issue. There has to be something else going on. I'll bet this is Tom's fault. Okay, so we made a mistake, but if the relationship were better, this one problem wouldn't have brought on such a severe response. Tom probably hasn't even visited MacroZip yet. I bet he isn't spending enough time and attention on the accounts that matter most. I told Peters he wasn't up to the job.* A plan was starting to take shape in her mind.

Chapter 5

Tom sat at his desk, phone held several inches from his ear, listening to Gary Howard at MacroZip Electronics rip him and Premiere to pieces. When he could squeeze a word or two into the pauses in Gary's tirade, Tom continued to apologize for the problem, offering to bring Premiere's entire management team over to meet with him and promising to do better in the future.

"I'm sorry I sent that e-mail," Gary said at last, running out of steam. "But I'm really furious! I'm in no mood for some dog-and-pony show from Peters and the rest of you guys. I don't want you in my building. I trusted you guys. I've even gone to bat for you guys with our CFO. We pay more for your service than your competitors. I did that because of your commitment to excellence. I hadn't realized you were relying on your reputation and that your quality had gone down. Look, I've worked with Premiere for a long time, and I *do* have some loyalty to our service providers. I *might* consider letting you stay, but the price I'm paying for the level of service I'm getting is simply too high. I would need a serious reduction in price even to consider retaining your company."

Tom was encouraged. This was the first sign of light in his twenty-five-minute conversation. "Thank you, Gary. I appreciate your understanding. Your business is important to us, and we've always tried to give you very competitive prices and provide the highest quality service."

"I don't know what your definition of *competitive* is, Tom. I know you're new to Premiere, but you've been around the business for a while. You and I both know that trucking is a commodity, and you're a premium-priced vendor. I'd need at least a 30 percent discount to consider keeping you around."

Tom stifled a gasp. There was no way Peters would go for a 30 percent discount. "Okay, Gary. I'll talk with Mr. Peters and get back to you. Thanks for being willing to work with us."

Tom spent the rest of the day working through possible scenarios to mitigate the 30 percent revenue hit, all the while pondering what it might take to sell his house on the hill and beg for his old job back.

With the parking lot nearly empty, no solution in sight, and the feeling that there'd be no peace at home tonight, Tom called an old buddy to go have a few beers.

"How Could This Happen?"

Chapter 6

"**H**ey, stuff happens. Get over it!" Vijay Patel, Tom's best friend, joked while commiserating with him at the bar late Monday night.

"Easy for you to say. I'm the one whose life's totally upside down," Tom lamented.

"Why is it upside down? From what you've said, you weren't the one who screwed up. Wasn't it Operations' fault?"

"It doesn't really matter. It means I have to go up against Carolyn Arnold. That's like taking on General Patton. She takes no prisoners! And Peters relies on her. They've been working together for something like twenty years. There's no way he's going to believe me over her. Worse, even if I win that political battle, I'm still saddled with the underlying problem.

I went to work at Premiere because of the company's reputation for great performance. Excellence has been their core differentiator for years. If customers start losing trust in Premiere's performance, I've got nothing to offer but high prices! How am I supposed to make quota with that offering?"

"There's no other way to set yourselves apart?" Vijay asked.

"I don't think so. The industry's pretty commoditized already. I've been amazed we've been able to sustain our leadership in operational excellence for as long as we have."

"So what are you going to do?"

"I have no idea right now. MacroZip's not only our biggest account; they're our flagship. They're our best reference, and if word gets out that MacroZip's dropping our services, we might lose a dozen other companies as well."

"Would they all really leave?" Vijay challenged his friend.

"No, probably not, at least not right away," he admitted. "But I wouldn't be surprised if we had a series of price renegotiations, drops in volume—you know, things like that. Most of our clients source from several vendors. It doesn't take long for a client to switch the volume of their business from one service provider to another. In fact, I'm probably more concerned about silent shifts in client behavior than I am about the tough negotiations we might have. I'm more worried about what I can't see than what I can see, if that makes sense."

"Have you told Trish?" Vijay asked, referring to Tom's wife.

"Unfortunately! She's freaked out about having to sell the house, the kids changing schools—like it's my fault."

"It *is* your fault!" Vijay teased.

"Thanks, man. You're a lot of help—but you know, it probably is my fault. I was the one who suggested stretching our budget to the limit to buy that stupid house. Now look where I am. You and I talked about Premiere before I went there. They had a great reputation. Customers liked their services. How hard would it be to sell that kind of product? Compared to where I was coming from, it seemed easy. It's a cakewalk to sell a product you believe in. I thought I'd achieve at least 125 percent of quota in my first year. But what if I was wrong? What if Premiere's service isn't as stellar as I thought? What do you do when you no longer believe in your product?"

"Are you really questioning the underlying performance of Premiere?"

"I don't know. My confidence has definitely been shaken. Carolyn's pretty sharp. But I was amazed she didn't even know we'd missed the delivery until I brought it up in our staff meeting. I am beginning to wonder if we even know whether our performance is as good as we think. What should I do?"

Vijay swept his hand around the room like a real estate agent showing off a beautiful new home. "You could work here. I saw a help wanted sign in the front window. Come on, Tom. Snap out of it, man! You're a VP now. Did you think it was really going to be easy? Why do you think you're getting paid those big bucks? Because being a vice president is hard—that's why!"

"Have you ever had to deal with this type of situation?" Tom asked.

"Of course, I work in high tech! We see this kind of problem all the time. I remember when eBay was getting ready to do an IPO.* People became excited about online auctions, and the site received tons of hits and tons of people using the service. The service was overwhelmed. As a result, site performance plummeted, and they got lots of negative press. It was a difficult time, but they survived it."

---

* Initial public offering (IPO)

"I remember that."

"In my company," Vijay continued, "we faced a similar problem. We'd been building a reliable product for years. We had a great reputation. Our customers loved us, the press loved us, and the stock analysts loved us. We'd driven down the cost of our technical support and the time our customers had to wait on hold—from eight minutes to less than two. Our customer satisfaction was through the roof, and our sales and marketing teams were pushing our customer service as a key benefit."

"That's kind of like our company. What happened?"

"Unfortunately, the same thing as you. Life. Murphy's Law. I don't know. Our engineers blew it. We had a problem with one of our components that caused intermittent power outages on our devices. Our techs couldn't find the problem for a few weeks. The Internet was littered with complaints about our company. The press got a hold of the story and creamed us. As a result, a ton of customers started to call, asking if their product had the same problem. This caused our hold times to skyrocket to thirty minutes or more. Our competitors smelled blood and began attacking us in the media and with our accounts. The stock and media analysts went negative on us, causing the stock to plummet over 40 percent. This caused a shareholder lawsuit that we're still fighting to this day. Think about how much we've spent recovering from this single situation. It happened over two years ago, and our stock's still recovering. We've wasted tons of management manpower on this issue, and it wasn't even that big a product problem."

"What d'you mean it wasn't a big problem?" Tom asked.

"In the grand scheme of things, the product issue was no big deal. It took us three weeks to find the source of the problem. Once we did, it only took a day to fix it, and the fix was easy for customers to implement. When all was said and done, it was a nonissue. It's not like the defect was killing our customers or something critical like that. We didn't even need to do a product recall. We never had a problem like that before or since. Yet, as I said, we're still suffering from it."

"Well, aren't you a real source of encouragement?" Tom chided ironically. "I've got a lot to look forward to!"

"Hey, suck it up! Like I said before, you're a VP now. Welcome to the club. You'd better get used to it."

"So what do you suggest for your old friend here?" Tom asked, really looking for some wise counsel.

"Every company faces the same kind of issue you're now facing. To me, this is not about your business. It seems more about corporate politics. Make sure this stuff doesn't stick to you, buddy. Be Teflon Man. You'd better dodge this one. Otherwise, that Carolyn woman is going to pin it on you. If you don't figure out how to duck, you'll be looking for work. I guarantee it! Now, put on a happy face, go home and

reassure your wife that everything will be fine.
You've been hiding out here far too long."

"Thanks," Tom said, swallowing down the last sip of
his beer.

Chapter 7

Tuesday wasn't shaping up to be any better than Monday for Tom Fredericks. After the meeting with Peters, he had forgotten to call Trish to let her know he still had a job. Tom also had forgotten to tell her he was going out with Vijay for drinks. Trish had spent all Monday anxious and fearful and had fallen asleep on the couch before Tom had returned home. She was awakened by the noise from the garage door as Tom parked his car. Her fear had now morphed into anger, and she took much of the remainder of the night to "express herself" clearly to him. As a result, Tom was exhausted and late for the emergency management meeting Peters had called. Peters was not one to be kept waiting.

"Thank you for joining us, Tom," Peters said sarcastically, as Tom quickly shuffled into the back of the room, trying to be inconspicuous. "Where are we?"

"Good morning, sir. Sorry I'm late. I talked with Gary Howard at MacroZip yesterday. I have good news and bad news." Tom paused to assess his audience's reaction.

"Don't set me up, kid. Just give me the facts," Peters barked.

Carolyn smiled to herself. *He's not only late, but childish, too! This will be easy.*

"Okay," Tom said. "The good news is MacroZip's willing to stay with Premiere as their trucking company. It took a long time to get there, but they do have some loyalty to us after all of our years of service."

"What's the bad news?"

"Gary was very discouraged with our performance. He was surprised how much it had slipped. We talked around the issue a while, but the basic conclusion he reached was to keep our business, we'll have to drop our prices 30 percent."

Premiere's financial manager, Anne Simpson, piped up instantly. "There's no way! We don't have those kinds of margins!"

"That's crap! Our performance hasn't declined!" shouted Carolyn Arnold. "Tom's simply too weak to stand up to MacroZip and do his job!"

"Okay, people. Calm down," Peters commanded. "Calm down!" Everyone got quiet. It was never a good idea to countermand Hank Peters.

"Anne, I understand your position and I agree. Consider it noted. But Carolyn, you've made a pretty bold assertion here. Prove to me that our performance hasn't gone down. The way I see it, MacroZip lost a client because we screwed up. Explain to me why that's not the case."

"With pleasure," Carolyn said, smirking at Tom. "I had the team stay up well into the night to analyze our performance for MacroZip Electronics over the last three years. I would go back further, but our information systems don't have the older data online. Here's what we found." Carolyn passed around a black-and-white graph of their performance. Using color would only have been gloating.

"As you can see here," she continued, pointing to the small dip at the end of a long positive trend line, "this is our first missed shipment in over nineteen months and only the third in three years. To put this in context, we have only had one shipment error in the last three thousand. That's a quality ratio of 99.97 percent. I'm sure we're far better than anyone else in our industry. The truth is our performance has been improving over the last year, not declining. Clearly, Operations didn't cause MacroZip to terminate the relationship. It's Sales." Carolyn was starting to build a case for Tom's removal.

"That's bull, and you know it!" Tom shouted, out of character. "I don't know if you're telling the truth about that performance or not, but it doesn't matter.

Clients like MacroZip certainly don't feel like we're providing such great service. If your team hadn't screwed up, we wouldn't be in this situation."

"Enough, *children*." Peters looked at both Carolyn and Tom. "All right. Carolyn, your crew blew it last week on that shipment. But I agree with you that something else must have happened to get a formerly good customer so hot. I need to spend some time thinking about this. I've got a call set up with Frank Sommers at the end of the day. In the meantime, you two stay here with Anne and work on how we get out of this mess. Understood?"

They all nodded apprehensively as Peters left the room.

Chapter 8

"I need a break!" Tom said to the two women after Peters left the room. "I'll be back in fifteen minutes." He picked up his coffee mug and stormed out the door.

Tom was red with anger. He was mad at himself for not seeing Carolyn's attack coming so quickly. Moreover, Tom had been in sales long enough to know when he was being fed propaganda. He wasn't going to instantly buy Carolyn's claims of excellent performance. He needed to validate the claims for himself. He secretly went to his office and spent the next twenty minutes talking with his own sales reps, truckers, and dispatchers. With mixed emotions, Tom learned that Carolyn was essentially correct. The feedback from his team and the frontline operations folks confirmed that Premiere's performance was good, even outstanding. *If we're doing such a good job, why did Gary Howard say our performance was declining? Why would we have to drop our prices so much? Is it all because of one mistake? It can't be. There has to be something else going on—some problem in Operations. It can't be Sales. I've known Gary for a long time, and he said explicitly it was an operations quality issue, not a sales issue. What am I missing?* Tom thought. Unfortunately, no answer was forthcoming.

"Oh! Thanks for joining us," Carolyn said to Tom as he reentered the conference room. She dramatically looked at her watch to highlight her displeasure with his late return.

Tom paused for a moment deciding what to say next. "Why do you think MacroZip wants to leave?" he said at last.

"Bad sales management. It has to be," Carolyn swiftly replied.

"Nice accusation. What evidence do you have it's a sales management problem?"

"Everything was fine before *you* got here."

"That's interesting . . . including performance?" he mocked. "It appears your quality has also gone down since I got here. Was that my fault, too?"

"Cut it out! We aren't getting anywhere," Anne interrupted. "Let's move on."

"Here's where I get lost. You say our performance is great, but our biggest customer doesn't think so. What happened to 'the customer's always right?'" Tom asked.

"That's only because you haven't managed the account well enough. If you had a better relationship with MacroZip, they wouldn't be leaving us," Carolyn replied.

"That's bull," he retorted. *I have a great relationship with Gary Howard,* Tom thought to himself. *I wonder if we were overselling our performance to him before I got here.* "How are we supposed to manage our accounts better?"

"They should know how good a company we really are," she answered. "We should be showing them our great performance."

"Fair enough. Let me ask you this, then. Where did these reports come from?" Tom asked Carolyn, pointing to the data she had just presented.

"They came from my department—my analysis," she replied.

"They're pretty impressive," Tom said. "They say a lot about how well we've been doing. How long have we been showing these reports to MacroZip?" Tom smiled inside. She was trapped. She would have to acknowledge she wasn't supplying the information he needed to manage the account. It was back on her.

"We haven't," Carolyn admitted. "We created those reports last night."

"Interesting. So what data have we been providing to MacroZip that highlights our great service?" Tom asked.

Carolyn saw the trap and tried to sidestep it. "They don't need these reports to know we're doing a good job. They already know. Our volume with them has been going up over the last year. Why would they have bought more of our services if our performance had been declining? It doesn't make sense," she replied. "We've had no reports until yesterday of any complaints from MacroZip in a long while. I know, we checked."

"Is that how we track our performance?" Tom probed. "By complaints?"

"Sure, it's the best way. Customers don't want to be bothered telling us every time we do something right. They expect us to do things right. The only practical way is to track complaints or billing disputes to evaluate our performance."

"So what do we send to MacroZip each month? I still don't understand how the customer knows we're doing a good job."

"I don't send them anything," Carolyn replied.

Anne broke into the conversation. "Let me answer this one. Carolyn doesn't create any account reports. My team does. Every month, we confirm which transactions we've completed for each customer, and then we send them a monthly activity report, which is included with the invoice indicating the services we've provided," Anne said. "That's what we've always done."

"So, the only way we know we've done a good job is the customer didn't complain or contest a bill? Okay, now I'm worried!" Tom said. "How many more MacroZips are out there? Are we really assuming that silence means the customer is happy? That's the only way we measure performance?"

"Of course not!" Carolyn barked back. "We have a whole slew of internal performance measures, such as on-time delivery, efficiency by driver—lots of ways. We watch these measures like hawks."

"Okay. Good. So we do have some evidence of our claims of high performance. Do we send those measures over to the customer?" he asked, already knowing the answer.

"No, that'd be silly. They don't want that level of detail. Those reports are for internal management purposes, not for customer distribution," Anne said.

"Also, we don't want that level of scrutiny on our internal operations," Carolyn added. "We don't need to provide customers that kind of data. We'd be so distracted handling their useless questions that we'd never get anything done. I don't need any micromanagement, thank you! Anyway, it's sales' responsibility to communicate this kind of stuff to our customers, not mine."

"Well, I don't remember seeing those reports. Do you normally send them to us in sales?" he asked.

"Not normally. Only when there's an issue," Carolyn replied.

"Interesting. Then how are we supposed to show our customers that we're doing a good job?" Tom asked again.

There was a long pause.

"This meeting has been very illuminating," Tom said at last. "No one's willing to admit it, but we aren't providing any data to our customers that actually prove we provide excellent service. In fact, if I understand correctly, Carolyn, your team had to stay up all night to determine whether we were really providing 'excellent' performance for MacroZip. And they're only one out of the hundreds of accounts we have. Everything we know about our performance is internally driven and kept inside your Operations Department. We aren't providing any information to our customers because you aren't providing any information to your own sales team. No wonder they think we're resting on our reputation!" Tom got up from his chair.

"We've got a real problem," he continued. "I heard what you said about our great service, but if excellence actually delivered 'victory' at Premiere, I wouldn't be losing my biggest customer over a performance issue. And I certainly don't feel victorious. That's for darn sure." With that, Tom turned around and walked out of the meeting.

Chapter 9

A flood of questions swirled in Hank Peters' head all morning, with no answers emerging. The typical stream of interruptions only intensified his confusion. By lunch, he knew he had to get out of the office to organize his thoughts. Peters picked up the phone and called Sam Clark, his former Marine captain who also happened to be his personal financial planner and best friend. "Sam, I need to get out of here. Can I buy you some lunch?"

Sam instantly knew something was wrong. Hank Peters never went out to lunch. "No, it sounds like you need more than lunch. I'm taking you golfing. It's been too long, and I think we need time to really talk. As your commanding officer, I won't take no for an answer. Grab your clubs and meet me at the golf course in an hour."

"Yes, sir!" Peters replied, smiling for the first time in days.

"Hank Peters," Hank said, introducing himself to the older married couple he and Sam had been paired with for the next eighteen holes.

"Darryl Jensen, and this is my wife, Nancy," the gentleman said, extending a hand.

"What do you do, Hank?" Nancy asked.

"I run a trucking company. How about you?" he replied.

"I'm mostly retired now. I used to be in politics—I was in Congress for a time. Now I sit on the boards of some charities," she said.

"That's different. I don't think I've ever met some-one from Congress in person. Nice to meet you," Peters replied.

"How about you Sam? What do you do?" she asked.

"I'm a financial planner. Darryl, how about you? What line of work are you in?" Sam asked.

"I'm retired, too. I used to run a company that provides technical services to small banks."

"Great," Sam replied. "Look forward to playing with you both."

After the foursome hit off the first tee, Sam pulled Peters aside and offered him a cigar. "Here. Have a smoke and talk to your old buddy."

Peters grabbed the cigar. "Thanks. I need one. It's been a tough couple of days, and the stuff that's been going on is going to impact what we've been talking about—my retirement situation."

"I thought that might be the issue," Sam said. "I know the schedule for possibly selling the company has been moved up, but don't worry. All of your retirement materials should be ready soon. If that big company wants to begin due diligence to buy your company, we'll be ready." He stopped to light up his cigar.

"Everything might be ready from your side, Sam, but not from my side. Anne's been doing an excellent job getting the books ready, but yesterday MacroZip, my largest account, just gave us a termination letter—e-mail, actually."

"Ah. Now I understand why you were upset this morning."

"It's a mess. It really is," Peters lamented.

"The timing isn't particularly good, I must admit," Sam chuckled, trying to lighten up his friend.

"You can say that again. MacroZip's our most profitable account. They represent 20 percent of our revenues but almost half of our profits. My business valuation will plummet if MacroZip terminates their relationship with us. I won't be able to sell the company at a high enough price to retire, and without

MacroZip, there won't be enough cash flow to enable Carolyn to do a management buy-out. It's totally messed up my plan. I promised myself I'd retire at sixty at the top of my career, and now look where I am."

"Playing golf?" Sam grinned with the cigar clenched in his teeth. "It feels like retirement. I don't understand your problem," he said in mock bewilderment.

"Seriously," Peters replied, trying to stifle a snicker.

"Sarge, I've known you forever. I know you want to retire in the next year, but you've got to slow down. I need to understand what's going on before I pass judgment on whether you'll have to work until you're seventy, . . . eighty, . . . you know, . . . whenever."

"Quit it," Peters laughed, giving his friend a shove. "You're really starting to tick me off. You're not very helpful." Peters spent the first nine holes walking Sam through the MacroZip situation and how it was inextricably linked to his retirement. Sam listened intently to Peters, while Peters concentrated on finding his way out of the rough.

By the turnaround—the "pit stop" between the first and second half of a round of golf—Darryl and Nancy Jensen heard enough of the conversation to understand why Hank Peters was playing so badly. "Do you mind if I offer some advice?" Darryl asked.

"I'm open to any suggestions, but nobody can fix my swing," Peters replied. It had been a tough round for Peters so far.

Darryl laughed. "Actually, I bet it's your company, not your swing, that needs fixing."

"Yeah, I guess you heard. I just didn't see this one coming . . ." Peters' discouraged voice quieted once Darryl placed his ball on the tee.

"I know exactly how you feel," Darryl said, hitting the ball straight down the fairway. "I've been there. I had a similar situation before I retired." Darryl waited quietly as Peters readied his tee shot.

"Really? In what way?" Peters asked, just after slicing his ball into the rough.

They started walking down the fairway. "Like you, I ran a specialty service business. I started to see increased turnover in our major accounts. When their contracts were up for renewal, some of our biggest customers started sending out requests for quotes—to several key competitors. For the first time, we had to compete to keep customers we'd had for years. In fact, we lost our first big customer in over ten years. It was a tough time."

"I can relate. Did you figure out what was going on?"

"Eventually, but it took a while," Darryl said, as Peters headed toward the rough to find his ball.

"I was thinking about what you said. Why would the customers all of a sudden start acting differently? Did you ever figure that out?" Peters asked, renewing the discussion with Darryl as they caught up to each other near the green.

"Customers thought we were taking them for granted—and, in an odd way, we were. We'd become complacent, thinking our customer relationships were permanent," Darryl said. "The scary part was the longer we'd worked with a client, the more likely they were considering a switch."

"That's fascinating. Was it laziness on the part of sales? Were they not managing the accounts correctly? Was it a prioritization issue? What was going on?" Peters probed. Peters thought about his own situation. *I wonder if Carolyn has been right about Tom all along. We hadn't had a problem with MacroZip until he got here.*

"We had the same questions. We thought it was a sales management issue at first, too. We created a major accounts team to deal with the issue, but it didn't help. All it did was increase our cost of sales.

The problem still remained. We figured it must be something else."

"Was it driven by competition or something else going on in the market?" Peters asked. "When I see clients starting to flee, it's usually because some competitor is trying to steal my accounts. They're out there bad-mouthing me to the industry. It happens all the time in my business. Does it happen in yours?"

"Sure. That was another place we looked. Was there a new competitor on the block? Were our existing competitors offering new features or benefits, things like that? However, we didn't find any major changes in our competitive situation. We weren't under attack in any abnormal way. And pricing was fine, too. We weren't in a price war with anyone. We were a little higher priced in general, but not enough to engender the kind of situation we were facing."

Peters mulled the situation over while walking to the next hole. *It has to have been a service performance issue,* Peters thought to himself. *Most companies don't*

*think hard enough about providing excellent service.
That's been the difference for us between winning and
losing customers.* "*Excellence Delivers Victory!*" The
irony of that thought was not lost on Peters. He
admitted to himself he wouldn't be in this situation if
Premiere's team hadn't botched the MacroZip shipment. *Maybe it's just that. Performance. Maybe I
haven't focused enough on it lately. Nah, it can't be our
performance. Provide great service, and customers stick
with you—that's my philosophy. And I trust Carolyn.
She says we've been doing a great job for MacroZip. I
don't understand what's up.* Peters kept mulling the
thoughts, like puzzle pieces, over and over in his
mind. Back and forth. Sideways. Upside down. It did-
n't matter. The pieces just didn't fit right. Something
was missing, but he couldn't put his finger on it.

"I hate to ask, but how good was your company's
performance?" Peters asked Darryl as they
approached the next tee box.

"It wasn't perfect, but our service record was pretty
high, one of the best in the industry. It was strange.

As we implemented quality improvement programs, our overall performance continued to improve, even as this problem was going on," Darryl said.

"My old commanding officer taught me that 'Excellence Delivers Victory!'" Peters said, smiling at Sam. "In warfare, without excellence, people die. Excellence has always been the guiding principle for our business."

"Pretty smart guy, that captain," Sam laughed, winking at his friend. "Pretty smart guy."

Darryl laughed, looked at Sam and said, "But not a great golfer."

"Good thing I'm not paid to be a golfing partner! As his financial planner, though, performance is pretty important. Friend or not, if I did a crappy job managing his money, I know he'd dump me."

"In a minute!" Peters replied. "Actually, Sam, I've been meaning to talk with you . . ." Peters joked.

"It's amusing to listen to you guys," Nancy Jensen said, joining the conversation. "Yet you warrior types are only seeing half the picture. All you talk about is performance, performance, performance. Listen, I was in Congress for twelve years, and I understand the political side to these types of situations. You talk about war. Well, war's messy. We all know it's messy. Excellence is critical to victory, of course. But it's not sufficient. You have to manage the public as well. When wars happen, people die. Even the best-trained and elite fighters have casualties. Even the biggest, most successful armies lose battles. The job of a politician is to get the public to be ready for those casualties and manage the public's expectations. Politics is all about managing expectations. Why would your world be any different?"

"You're absolutely right!" Sam marveled. "I hadn't thought of it that way."

"Is your wife right?" Peters asked. "Are we missing the big picture?"

"Hank, that's a tricky question for a man to answer *in front* of his wife." Darryl laughed and smiled at Nancy. "Actually, as always, she's dead on. At my company, our obsession with continuous process improvement had yielded better service. As we progressed, the smaller problems started to disappear. We kept getting better and better. Unfortunately, when we did have a problem, it tended to be pretty noticeable. We'd assemble a highly visible team to resolve the problem, causing the spotlight to fall on these large but rare problems rather than our typically excellent service. Our good service had made us relatively invisible. But our clients had lost track of our overall excellent performance and began focusing on each individual problem. When our contracts were up for renewal, our customers still focused on the issues that *we'd* made most visible: the problems, not on our total performance. It was frustrating."

"I know where you're coming from," Peters commiserated. "It seems that people like to dwell in the here and now."

"That's pretty common in politics," Nancy said. "Voters have short memories. It's not only critical to give them what they want. You have to time it. If you give them what they want too early in your term, they'll forget what you did and still demand more. Otherwise, you'll lose the election."

"Which is why she's here playing golf," Darryl kidded. "Anyway, like Nancy was saying, as we improved our service, our customers lost sight of our value. The better we got, the more invisible we became. Except when there was bad news."

"You're right. That's it! We have the same problem," Peters exclaimed. "Everybody takes us for granted. When I think about this situation I'm facing, it makes me mad. I know we've been a great vendor for MacroZip. Our level of service has been out-standing. We have very strong processes and pro-cedures. We did everything we could to deliver their product on time. Yet still they want to get rid of us."

Nancy interjected, "I think this invisibility idea is true for every organization. I now sit on the board of a large local charity, and we face this issue every day. We've been doing our job successfully for over fifty years, and we're really good at it. But no one notices us. We're invisible to the community. It's another thing I learned in politics. Invisible is not a good state to be in. Invisible people don't get reelected, and invisible charities don't get donations," Nancy said.

"For politics, that makes sense, but how does it apply to charities?" Sam asked.

"With charities, if you advertise, you increase people's awareness of what you're doing, which raises visibility. That's good. However, people then think you're wasting money and not spending it on direct programs for the charity. It really creates a paradox," Nancy explained.

"Yeah, I hadn't thought of it that way, but it most certainly is a paradox," Darryl agreed. "Until I heard

you sharing your frustration with Sam earlier, I
thought that the situation we'd faced was unique.
However, as we've all been talking, I'll bet there are
a lot of other organizations facing Nancy's paradox."

Peters' game continued to falter as he pondered the
paradox they had just uncovered. His mind continued to race, trying to resolve it. This had not helped
his game at all. He finished the round with his worst
score in a decade.

"I don't want to be invisible. I want to be recognized for the great work my company does," Peters
said over drinks at the clubhouse. "I don't like being
taken for granted."

"Who does? Joanne didn't," Sam replied, sticking it
to Peters.

"Ouch, that hurts," Peters mocked, pretending he
had received a stab wound in the chest.

"Who's Joanne?" Darryl asked.

"Joanne is Hank's first wife—his ex-wife, I should say. They broke up while we were in the Corps together," Sam explained.

"The reason Sam chose this time to dredge up such wonderful memories is because the reason she left was because I 'took her for granted.'"

"Ouch is right!" Nancy said, rolling her eyes toward her husband and arching her brows. "I think we've all felt that way at one point in time, hmm?"

"But that was a long, long, long time ago," Darryl replied with a big smile.

On the drive back from the course, Peters called his old friend and customer, Frank Sommers, MacroZip's COO. He briefly explained what happened to the wayward shipment, apologized, and asked, as a friend, to be given a few weeks before MacroZip made any final decisions about keeping Premiere. To Peters' relief, Sommers agreed.

Next, Peters scheduled another emergency management meeting for early Wednesday morning. He knew the meeting with the potential acquirers of Premiere was three weeks away. He had to fix this problem, and fast.

Chapter 10

Tom Fredericks battled the fog to arrive at work early Wednesday morning. Yesterday, he had met late in the day with Anne and Carolyn, with nothing but a migraine to show for it. Both women had stonewalled Tom at every turn. As the financial manager, Anne Simpson knew Peters' retirement plans intimately. She knew Carolyn Arnold might soon become her next boss and had chosen sides quickly between Carolyn and Tom. Carolyn was committed to pushing Tom quickly out the door. The situation with MacroZip was simply an opportune vehicle.

By the time he'd arrived home Tuesday night, Tom was tired and frustrated, and Trish was completely unsympathetic. Tom had convinced her that he could handle their great lifestyle leap and had accepted that it was now his primary responsibility to keep the money coming in. Tom knew she was thinking this and that she was right, but that didn't make it any easier. As a result, Tom hadn't slept much and had headed into the office early to avoid being late two days in a row. He was tired, grumpy, and visibly stressed.

"Morning," Peters grumbled to the team as he entered the meeting room. He also had slept terribly the night before, tossing and turning and trying to make sense of his situation.

"I played golf with Sam Clark yesterday," Peters said, signaling the start of the emergency meeting.

Each person reacted uniquely to the news.

I wonder if Sam Clark liked my materials for the acquisition, Anne thought.

Are they moving up the schedule? Perfect, Carolyn thought. *I hope Peters and Clark worked out the details of my buy-out.*

Why was Peters playing golf instead of figuring out how to fix the problems with operations? Tom thought.

Being relatively new to Premiere, he was totally
unaware of any back-room dealings. He didn't know
who Sam Clark was, and he had no idea about the
possible acquisition or management buy-out.

"We had an excellent discussion about the situation
with MacroZip," Peters said, dispelling each person's
assumptions about the golf game. "Sam and I met
an interesting couple. The guy, Darryl Jensen, is a
former CEO, and his wife is a former Congress-
woman who sits on the board of directors for a
big local charity. They each described circumstances
that matched almost exactly what's happening
with us."

"In what way were they similar?" Carolyn asked.

"According to you, Carolyn, our performance has
been improving—the best in the industry. Yet our
largest customer wants to leave us over one mistake.
That doesn't make much sense, does it?" he asked.

"Not really," she admitted.

"Yesterday, I learned that our excellent performance could actually be causing the problems we're now facing." Peters could see from the looks on everyone's faces that what he had just said still didn't make any sense. They didn't know what to say next.

"What do you mean?" Carolyn challenged him. "Are you suggesting our performance is too good? I don't understand."

"Not exactly. Last night I puzzled over the seeming paradox that both our company and Darryl's have experienced. Like us, they found themselves with a reputation for excellence, but facing customer defections. Then I got it on the way to work this morning. Both companies have encountered what I now call the *paradox of excellence*. Let me explain. The paradox of excellence is this: As our performance improves, we become more invisible to our customers—to everything but bad news. As a consequence, customers lose sight of the true value we deliver because they forget the problems we eliminate. The reality is strange, but true. I think this applies to us. We've become invisible to most of our clients. Does anyone disagree with that assertion?"

Everyone shook their heads, but without much conviction. It still sounded like Peters was telling them that the reason MacroZip had a problem with Premiere was because their performance had been too good. Peters continued, "Okay, stay with me on this. Who believes we're invisible to MacroZip today?"

For the first time in days, laughter broke out. "Okay. I see what you mean," Carolyn admitted. "When you're doing a really great job, the only time the customer notices you is when you have a problem."

"Correct. Also, when you think about it, even the smallest amount of light shined in a pitch-black room can be blinding. We've done such a good job for our customers for so long, they've come to expect it. Our great service is no longer extraordinary, just expected. We're invisible. Now, because we've been invisible to our customers for a long time, even the smallest problems seem enormous," Peters said.

"This is clearly the situation with MacroZip. They don't know how good they have it. That's why they're so disappointed in what happened."

"And that's why they want a discount," Tom added.

"Exactly," Peters said. "Now this all makes sense to me. Does it make sense to you folks?"

"It definitely makes sense to me," Tom said. "We were talking about that very topic after our meeting yesterday."

"I don't know what's causing the paradox, but it's important that we dig deeper," Peters urged.

"I agree. We shouldn't just trust our gut on this," Carolyn interjected. "Let's get some facts behind the situation and really see what's going on."

"I feel the same way," Peters said, pausing to collect his thoughts. "Here's what we're going to do. I've talked with MacroZip and asked them to give us a few weeks to come up with a plan to keep their business, and they've agreed."

There was a collective sigh of relief.

"In the meantime, Tom, I want you to survey some customers to gather their perceptions of our performance. I also want to see some competitive analysis. Carolyn, I want to see our operational performance, by account. Let's meet next Monday at our regular management meeting time, and we better have some answers. Understood?"

"Yes," they all agreed.

Chapter 11

"Clue me in here," Tom asked his sales rep, Ryan, after he left the meeting. "Who's Sam Clark?"

"You don't know?" Ryan couldn't believe it.

"Peters mentioned him in the management meeting today. I've never heard of him."

"He's Peters' retirement planner," Ryan said, as if it were obvious.

"Oh no," Tom groaned. The pieces began to fall into place. "Why did Peters meet him yesterday?"

"You know that Peters is thinking of retiring, right?" Ryan asked hesitantly, trying not to make his boss feel left out.

"Of course, eventually."

"Sure, if eventually means in the coming year."

"I was afraid you'd say that," Tom said. "Get in there." Tom pointed to his office.

"Okay. Spill," Tom said, after closing the door to his office.

"Anne told me that Peters was going to retire soon—probably next year. I don't know if it's true, but it wouldn't surprise me," Ryan said.

"What do you think will happen then?" Tom asked.

"I guess Carolyn will run the company. She pretty much runs most of it already."

Damn! Tom thought. *I knew it! Ugh!* "What else have you heard?"

"Not much. I'm just a sales guy. All I know is things are 'a brewin'' as they say, and the MacroZip situation hasn't helped a bit."

The phone on Tom's desk rang, interrupting their clandestine discussion. "Okay, scram!" Tom directed Ryan.

Tom turned on his sales charm. "This is Tom Fredericks. How may I help you?" he asked the person on the phone.

"Tom, Kathy Martin—good to hear your voice." Tom grimaced at the sound of her voice. Kathy Martin was his arch-nemesis at Jumbo, the logistics company he had left only a month ago. *Man, it seems like forever ago,* he thought. Kathy was now running Tom's old sales team.

"Kathy. Good to hear your voice," he said with fake enthusiasm. "What can I do for you?"

"I was just calling to reconnect, as I hear we might be working with you again soon."

Tom's guard immediately went up. He had not told anyone except Vijay about possibly going back to

Jumbo, and Vijay could keep a secret. He didn't know how Kathy knew he had been thinking about going back. "What do you mean, Kathy?"

"From what I hear, Jumbo is making a bid on Premiere. Rumor has it that Jumbo is meeting with Hank Peters in a few weeks to talk about buying up your little company. It's funny. Just think about it. In a couple of weeks, you could be working for me!" Kathy gloated with obvious pleasure. Tom was floored. He couldn't believe it. There was no way he'd be kept on board if they merged the two companies. "You shouldn't believe everything you hear!" Tom lamely countered. Before she could reply, Tom continued, "Look, I've got to go. Good talking with you, Kathy." Tom hung up the phone and kicked his trashcan. No, he was definitely not having a good day.

Chapter 12

Carolyn walked out the back door of the building to have a cigarette. Her head was spinning. There was a lot happening all at once. The entire week had gone sideways. She was angry that Tom hadn't simply come to her with the MacroZip issue before bringing it up in the management meeting. She had been thinking a lot about what Tom had said. *He's not completely wrong,* she thought. *In fact, he's not wrong at all. Maybe he's not as stupid as I thought.*

If she were fully honest with herself, her team had blown it several ways. First, her team should have notified her first thing Monday morning about the debacle with Single. Carolyn was mad at herself because the existing system was not real-time enough. She received her weekend report Monday afternoon, not Monday morning. That would definitely be fixed.

Second, Carolyn was furious it had taken all night to build the case supporting their excellent performance. The data had not existed in a format that was useful for management, let alone for a customer. She wasn't quite willing to share that realization with Tom just yet, but she admitted he was right about it. It angered her, but the Information Technology team was under Anne, and Carolyn didn't want to make too many enemies at once. She needed Anne's support until the buy-out was consummated.

Third, and most worrisome, was the underlying notion that her raison d'être, her reason for being, was crumbling. From a big-picture perspective, Premiere's performance was exemplary. Yet, here she was, head of operations, heir apparent to run the company—and she wasn't sure that performance was going to carry them forward for the next twenty years. Tom had raised the issue of perception and so had Peters. *This paradox of excellence idea of Hank's might have some merit,* Carolyn mused, puffing silently in the afternoon sun.

Maybe I've been too hard on Tom, she decided at last. *I can't have him leave anytime soon. With MacroZip gone, it'd be hard to get another VP of sales. Plus, if marketing and sales are going to become more important to our company's future, I'd better have someone covering that area at all times when I become CEO. I can't have him quit and leave me to oversee sales, too!*

"Time to go in and start the marathon," Carolyn said out loud, throwing her spent cigarette onto the sidewalk and stamping it out with her shoe. Carolyn knew her team would have to work all weekend to prepare the reports Peters had asked for. The next several days were going to be very long indeed.

The Way Out

Chapter 13

Vijay visited Tom's house Wednesday night to discuss Tom's career strategy. Tom was in a difficult spot. With what he had learned over the last couple of days, Tom had come to the realization he would probably not be the next CEO of Premiere. In fact, he might never be CEO anywhere. He was furious that Hank Peters had not disclosed his retirement plans during Tom's recent recruitment to Premiere. However, Tom and Vijay had talked about whether he should confront Peters about the oversight, and they decided that right now, Tom should stay focused on keeping his job, making his numbers, and finding a way out of the crisis they were in. He'd confront Peters about his retirement after Tom had saved the relationship with MacroZip. Also, he realized he had no choice but to support Carolyn and try saving his career. It was a bitter pill, which, with Vijay's coaxing, Tom duly swallowed.

On the way into work Friday morning, Tom swung over to the bagel shop to pick up a peace offering for Carolyn. Once at the office, he stopped at Carolyn's door and poked his head in. "Truce?" he asked, leading with the bagels.

Carolyn laughed cautiously. "Truce."

"Look, I didn't mean to put you on the defensive the other day," he said. "I'm sorry."

"I understand. Apology accepted. We've both got a lot at stake here. In the future, though, if you have an issue with my group's performance, come see me first, not Peters. Okay?"

"Fair enough. Bagel?" Tom asked, offering up the bag.

"Don't mind if I do." Carolyn reached into the bag and pulled one out.

Tom reached in next to get a bagel. "What do you think of this paradox thing Peters talked about yesterday?"

"Good question. I've been thinking a lot about that . . ., and about what you said the other day. I think they're linked."

"How so?" Tom asked, spreading cream cheese on his bagel.

"The paradox seems to have two dimensions, from what I can tell." Carolyn got up from her desk and went to the white board. She drew two boxes. "First is the notion of performance, and the second relates to perception."

"I would agree."

"I'm beginning to see that we spent a lot of time on the first box and not enough time on the second," Carolyn conceded.

"We can't succeed without having great performance. We both know that. I agree, though, that we need more balance. We need to raise the visibility of that great performance. We have to make people conscious of it. You see, it's not enough to have great performance; our customers have to value it, too."

"True. What I don't understand is why our customers don't automatically value what we're doing. They've told us what they want in terms of performance. For years, we've given them what they wanted. The whole situation with MacroZip has me a little mystified. I still haven't figured out why MacroZip suddenly wants to leave us—why they had so little loyalty."

"Me neither."

The two spent a couple of moments in silence, each chewing on the peace offering, while trying to put it all together.

"I've got to go make some customer calls," Tom said at last, standing up to leave. "But let's agree that this time, we'll coordinate our presentations."

"Good idea," Carolyn agreed. "Good idea."

Chapter 14

"Peters," Hank growled into his phone. It was just after lunch, and his to-do list was growing exponentially.

"Well Sarge, don't you sound chipper today!" Sam Clark laughed at his friend.

"What's up, Captain?" Peters replied. "I'm really swamped."

"I've been thinking a lot about that paradox we talked about the other day."

"Me too. I put a name to it: the paradox of excellence. The better you perform, the more invisible you become." Peters laughed. "Except, of course, when there's bad news."

"That's a great way to describe what Nancy Jensen said about expectations. I think she was onto something, and it sounds like you are, too," Sam said.

"Maybe. I'm not sure. I feel like I understand the symptoms. Unfortunately, I haven't been able to find the cause—or the cure."

"I might have found the cause," Sam said. "That's why I'm calling."

"Well? Are you going to tell me or leave me hanging?"

"Hmm, good question," Sam hesitated just to mess with his friend. "Some of what I learned while at the Pentagon finally clicked. Let me explain. You and I've been in a few firefights, haven't we?"

"That we have, Sam. That we have."

"During those firefights, how much of the big picture did we see?" Sam asked.

"Almost none. We had very little visibility on the overall picture. You know as well as I do, we were often in the 'fog of war.'"

"Exactly. The immediate circumstances dominated our thinking. It was hard to see how our firefight related to the overall battle we were fighting. Isn't that true?"

"Yes. Only Command and Control had the entire view of the battlefield."

"Right. Only they had the ability to put our firefight into the context of the entire battlefield. When I got promoted to the Pentagon, I realized for the first time that Congress and the public faced the same problem—how to evaluate the situation."

"Go on," Peters implored.

"So stop and think about it for a moment. If Congress were to ask how a war was going while we were in a firefight, what would you tell them?" Sam asked.

"Rough going, I guess."

"And you'd be right—from that perspective. But in the context of the entire war, that statement might not be true at all."

"Okay. I'm following."

"It's the same with customers, isn't it? If you ask a customer what they think about your service *while* you are providing bad service, what do you think they'd say?

"That we provide bad service," Peters replied.

"Exactly. They're witnessing a problem—a firefight—and they can't see beyond that fight to the overall situation. Their perspective is limited to that specific firefight. They don't have a comprehensive context in which to evaluate your performance."

"I'm with you."

"Think about it this way. If you supply excellent service, that service often becomes invisible. I agree with that concept. Now, let's say something bad happens. It's like the firefight example. Let's say your troops have been successfully winning ground in a war. However, the faster those troops won that ground, the more invisible their performance became. The Congress or the public began to expect that level of performance indefinitely. That success in gaining ground was less valued because capturing that ground was routine—it was expected. Are you with me?"

"I'm with you," Peters replied.

"Then, suddenly, a problem emerges. Just like your paradox of excellence predicts. There's a firefight. Somebody shoots at those troops. At the moment when it becomes visible, Congress or the public isn't thinking about the ground the troops have covered. They are not thinking about how well the war has been waged so far. They only see the crisis of the moment. Nonetheless, success or victory is not just in the immediate moment. They've lost sight of the overall time horizon. The firefight has to be kept in a broader, wider context. It takes seeing things from the top to put the specific firefight into the context of the overall battlefield, of the overall war."

"Interesting way of putting it," Peters said. "What do you suggest I do?"

"Let's talk through this. You continue to provide better service. Right?"

"Of course," Peters replied.

"How do your customers know you're providing better service?"

"I've been thinking about that a lot this week. I don't really know. If you'd asked me a week ago, I would have had a great answer. But this week, I don't know."

"Does your industry have a standard for how companies are judged?" Sam asked.

"No, not really. I think the criteria that customers use are not very defined."

"Here is where I make the connection," Sam continued. "Your company is the military in my example. You are the ones in the firefight. Your customer is like Congress or the public. They're the ones who have the wrong time horizon. They're the ones who have no visibility on the overall battlefield. They don't have any point of reference at all. Do they?"

"No. They don't."

"Why don't they?" Sam asked rhetorically, and then began answering his own question. "They don't have any point of reference because Command and Control hasn't given them one. In the military example, the leadership hasn't given visibility on the entire situation to Congress or to the public. The military leadership hasn't provided the overall context by which the current firefight can be evaluated. Without that context, the public simply assumes the worst-case scenario: they assume the current crisis represents the likely future outcome of the conflict. Does that make sense?"

"Yeah, I'm tracking with you."

"So let's bring it back to your company's current situation. You've been fighting to provide the best service in your industry. Unfortunately, you had a problem. Your customer—in this case, MacroZip—will always use the current crisis to judge your company's performance unless they appreciate all the great performance that came before. Your overall performance has to be kept visible."

"You know, you're right!" Peters said. "Customers only see the current crisis—the current firefight."

"Bingo. What's worse is, as your performance gets better, the expectations will also grow. Sometimes the expectations even grow faster than the performance. It's like that old song, 'What have you done for me lately?'"

"I get it. If we allow our customers to define the criteria by which we're evaluated, we give them too much control over how they view us."

"Exactly. See the connection? *You* are Command and Control. You see the big picture. And like Command and Control, you are responsible for keeping the overall picture clear in the mind of your customer. The root cause of the paradox of excellence, as you call it, is *you* have forced your customers to determine how to put your performance in context. You have not given them any context, so they're compelled to make up their own context in ways that are not always in your favor. This is how good companies lose customers. This is where customer loyalty gets lost."

"I think I finally understand. Customers want to have hope that the current crisis is an anomaly and not the future norm. It's our job to give it to them."

"Now you're thinking."

"Remember the other day when you said you were pretty smart?" Peters asked.

"Yeah," Sam answered.

"Well, finally I concur."

Chapter 15

As usual, the Monday 11 A.M. management meeting started right on time. "Well, team, what have we learned? Carolyn, you first."

"Actually, Tom and I worked together to combine our analyses," Carolyn said.

Peters smiled to himself. *Hmm . . . cooperation. Where'd that come from?* "Okay, then. Both of you, what do you have?"

Tom walked to the head of the table and put up an overhead slide. "If you look at the slide, the top line represents the opinion of our customers five years ago, the last time we did a satisfaction survey, and the next line displays the data from last week's interviews. As you can see, the perception of Premiere has declined substantially." He pointed to the 20 percent drop in the average opinion score.

Peters was shocked by the data. "How you do explain that?" he asked Tom.

"It was a surprise to me, sir," Tom replied. "I asked around quite a bit about Premiere's reputation before coming to work here. The perception in the industry, I thought, was very high."

"Well then, what the heck's going on?" Peters demanded.

Tom explained, "When this question was asked five years ago, we measured if customers thought our performance was above average, average, or below average. In that earlier study, most of our customers said we were above average. In last week's study, customers still like us, but now consider us just average. We've clearly lost our edge."

"Why do you think that's happened?" Peters probed.

"I don't think our competitors have improved that much, but rather our customers' expectations have risen," Tom suggested.

"I think so, too," Peters admitted. "I've been thinking about that all weekend."

"Yes. That's definitely possible—and maybe our performance helped to raise them," Carolyn added. "Take a look at these data. The line on the bottom, using the axis on the right, shows our aggregate performance level, which has been rising steadily over the same time frame." Carolyn pointed to a measure of overall delivery timeliness.

"As we expected," Peters replied. "It shows the paradox, doesn't it? Perceptions are declining while performance is improving."

"Yes it does," Tom and Carolyn both replied. The others also agreed.

"Okay. We're not done here. I gave you another task. Tom, did your team review the competition and get any competitive benchmarks on their performance levels?"

"It took a little while, sir, but I did find some benchmarks from the trade association."

"And?" Peters asked impatiently.

"Sure enough, we still have the best performance in the industry. Actually, by a fair margin," Tom said.

"It's true then, isn't it?" Peters asked. "We suffer from this paradox of excellence."

Heads nodded.

"Now what should we do about it?" he asked rhetorically. He continued without pause. "I've been thinking about what causes the paradox of excellence. Let me walk you through my thoughts, and then let's brainstorm about this." Peters took the next half hour to walk the team through the discussion Sam and Peters had on Friday, as well as the thinking Peters had done since then.

Chapter 16

As the team broke for lunch, Hank Peters went to the telephone. During the brainstorming session that just occurred, Peters realized he didn't know how to solve the paradox. He decided that during lunch he would seek out Darryl Jensen and see if he could help.

"Mr. Jensen," Peters said, talking on the telephone. "I don't know if you remember me, but my name's Hank Peters, and I played golf with you last Tuesday."

"Of course I remember you," he chuckled. "The 'Trucking Marine.' What can I do for you?"

"You talked about the situation at your company—that paradox you faced. After looking into our situation more deeply, it appears we suffer from the same condition. I was wondering if you could give me some hints on how you cured it."

"Sure. Let me tell you what happened in our situation. It took a while, but I realized our customers couldn't calibrate how much we were doing for them. We were providing excellent service but not making our improvements obvious to our customers. If I had to sum it up, we had to make our invisible, high-quality service visible to our customers," Darryl said.

"Make the invisible visible—that's it?" Peters queried.

"Actually it's more than that. We needed to provide continuous positive reinforcement of our distinguishing value. Service companies like ours deal with the ethereal, the abstract. We realized our company hadn't done enough to expose our distinctive level of performance to our customers," Darryl explained.

"Why do you think that was?" Peters asked.

"There are a couple of reasons. First, we thought far more about communicating with prospects than with our long-term customers. Second, we assumed customers observed our improvements in service and recognized how superior we were compared to the rest of the market. We forgot our customers needed context for evaluating our performance. The longer a customer stayed with us, the more difficult it was to put our performance into some comparative context."

Turning it back on Peters, Darryl said, "Let me ask you, Hank. How do you reinforce your value to your customers?"

"Good question. I've been thinking about that a lot since our last conversation. Our customers interact with us every day. They meet our drivers, talk with our customer reps, and interact with our accounting department. Unfortunately, the more I've thought about it, the less I think we provide any real reinforcement of our value."

"Your situation, like mine, is all too typical, I'm afraid," he said.

"What a mine field!"

Darryl chuckled. "Once a Marine, always a Marine! We divided the problem into three questions: First, were we providing what customers valued? Second, was our performance superior? Third, how should we reinforce our value? We knew from customer interviews we were providing a superior, high-performance service. For us, the key was to establish visibility of our value on an ongoing basis to our important customers. From a practical sense, this meant redesigning some IT systems and reports we originally provided only to our sales team and creating new marketing materials."

Peters thought about Darryl's comments for a moment. "Okay, let me see if I understand what you recommend. We should continuously communicate what's unique and relevant about what we provide to our customers. Is that correct?" he asked.

"I couldn't have said it better myself." Darryl said. "Now, I know every business situation is different. There are myriad ways to define and reinforce value. You need to be sure to find a smart way to reinforce that value that is socially acceptable. You also need to understand how to define your unique value—your core point of service differentiation."

"I really appreciate your time," Peters said, reviewing the notes he had taken. "One more thing. Where should my company go from here? Any suggestions?"

"I'd suggest you have your team look at service companies Premiere buys from and see whether you can discern what makes them excellent—how they compare themselves or manage your expectations, and how they reinforce their value. I'm sure the exercise will give you useful insights as to what's relevant to your business. And you, Hank, ought to get on the phone and talk with customers. You should confirm whether you're on the right track with your services. Are your services still relevant? Are they still unique? This is critical, and you should handle those calls personally."

"Will do, Darryl. Many thanks," Peters said.

Chapter 17

ank Peters called the team back into the meeting room. He went to a flipchart and drew
three columns with the following headings: "Service
Companies," "Their Unique Value," and "How They
Reinforce That Value."

The team shuffled back in, took their places around
the table, and looked up at what Peters wrote. "Have
a seat. Let's get started," Peters said. "I have an exercise we can do to understand better how we solve the
paradox of excellence."

"Let's list the service vendors we use here at Premiere. Anne, you're probably best suited to tell us
who they are," Peters said, handing the marker to his
head of finance.

Anne began listing a wide range of companies,
including telecommunication vendors, banks, credit

services, leasing firms, employment firms, and outside auditors.

"Good start, Anne. Can we think of any more?" Peters asked.

"We use marketing service firms like advertising, PR, web developers . . . a whole bunch of providers," Tom said.

"Good, Tom. Anyone else?" Peters asked.

"We use a local repair service for our fleet," Carolyn added.

"We use FedEx in sales, and we use a sales training company as well," Tom added.

After about fifteen minutes, the list had grown quite long. There were over fifty different service firms listed, including consultants, law firms, creative service agencies, furniture rental, IT outsourcing, cleaning services, and many others.

"Okay, we've assembled a pretty good list of service companies. Now let's talk about what makes them excellent. What's their value-add—what makes them different? Anne, why do we use our long-distance telephone company instead of their competitors?" Peters asked.

"They put together an overall package designed for trucking services like ours, which gave us the best price," Anne said.

"Good. We know their unique value—customized, competitively priced service for truckers. Let's do another. Anne, talk to me about your outside auditors."

"The main reason we picked them was they had some experience with companies such as ours. They had handled auditing services for three other shipping companies."

"How do you know they're still the best for us?" Peters asked.

"That's not a fair question to ask," Anne said defensively. "I've worked with them for years, and I've never had any problems."

"Anne, relax, I'm not going to ask you to switch. I simply want to know whether we have any way to evaluate their performance now in comparison to others."

Anne settled down and gathered her thoughts and emotions. "Sorry, boss. I like these guys. But I must admit, I don't know if they're any more experienced than other possible providers. It's been a long time since we did the comparison."

"Apology accepted. Does everyone see where I am going with this exercise?" Peters asked.

They all nodded.

"Okay, then. I'm going to get on the phone and call some of our larger customers to get some direct feedback. In the meantime, continue with this ex-

ercise. I want you to really think about how companies demonstrate excellence and how companies
reinforce that excellence to their customers. Really
push the envelope. Don't just consider work-related
services but any service you use at work or at home.
I especially want to understand how people reinforce
and communicate their value. I'll be back at the end
of the day to review your efforts."

Chapter 18

The conference room looked like a war room. Coffee cups covered the table, and the flipchart was black with notes. The air had turned stale by the time Hank Peters had returned.

"Looks like you've all been busy," Peters observed with a grin. "I have, too. Let me walk you through my calls, and then you can show me where we are."

He continued, "Over the last four hours, I've talked with almost a dozen of our largest customers. I must tell you, it was eye-opening. If I learn nothing else from this crisis, I'll walk away knowing I need to talk with our customers more often. I've spent so much time on operational issues that I'd forgotten how illuminating a simple conversation with a customer could be. I won't bore you with the details of the calls right now, I'll just share some of my conclusions."

Peters walked to the flipchart and turned to a clean page. "Our customers like us. They say we're the best in the industry—especially at delivering product within a very narrow band of time. From their point of view, being able to deliver in a tight window is definitely our key benefit. Do you agree?" Peters asked.

Everyone agreed.

Peters wrote "able to deliver in a tight window" on the flipchart page. "Okay, then. The key now is how we communicate that value to our customers. Have you created some examples for us to discuss?"

The team looked to Tom Fredericks, who had been compiling a final list from the chicken scratch on the flipchart. "Yes, sir. Let me walk you through our thinking process, and then let me give you some of our examples."

Peters smiled to himself. *Smart kid*. "Go ahead," he growled impatiently, to maintain his image.

"We started to build a list of ways companies can achieve excellence. It took a little while at first, but then the floodgates opened. Here are some ways service companies differentiate: price, quality, timeliness, scale, accuracy, friendliness, expertise, innovation, reliability, authenticity, completeness or selection, availability . . ."

"What do you mean by scale?" Peters interrupted.

"Scale could be the size of the offering. For example, if you go shopping at a large home improvement center like Home Depot, you might select them over the local hardware store because they have a huge selection. Their scale is enormous."

"Okay, good enough," Peters responded. "Give me some examples of expertise."

"Let's say you have cancer. You might go to a local hospital for treatment. However, you might go to the Mayo Clinic because they have the expertise in your particular form of cancer."

"Fine. Now talk about reinforcement. Give me some examples of that."

"I know this is outside our industry, but we thought of Albertson's, the grocery chain. They're a good example of saving money," Tom said.

"How so?" Peters pushed back.

"Have you ever shopped at Albertson's, sir?"

"Yeah."

"Well, when you use one of their loyalty cards that gives you a discount, . . . after you pay, they hand you your receipt, circle the amount you saved, and say 'Mr. Peters, you just saved $7.31 with your Preferred Card. Have a great day!' They reinforce their value—saving you, the customer, money every time you use their card."

"All right, give me another," Peters demanded.

"Google, the search engine. They actually have two attributes, speed and completeness. If you do a search on Google, they tell you how many web sites they found and how quickly. For example, I typed in "Premiere," and Google found 6.5 million web sites in less than a third of a second. They are reinforcing the completeness of their service within a set time frame. Pretty cool."

"Okay, another," Peters pushed.

"We looked at results—companies that focus on promising some outcome—and we found several interesting examples. Anne came up with the idea of private schools and their test scores. Each year, schools show how many graduates went on to big-name schools, what their average SAT scores were, the number of national merit scholars, you name it. They want to show the benefit of their school. Another example we came up with is Weight Watchers. At Weight Watchers, you get positive reinforcement for every five pounds you lose, and you also get a golden key when you achieve your goal weight. The golden key is a visual reminder of your success," Tom said.

"Actually, when you think about it, my gym does the same thing. They keep a record of my efforts and my performance. I can track how strong I'm getting over time. I hadn't thought about that until just now. Hmm. Very interesting. Okay, give me another," Peters said.

"Another is flexibility or responsiveness. We thought of Dell Computer. With Dell you get a low-cost product, but it's customized for you. You can go right on their web site, make your own product, and actually track its status at the factory," Tom continued.

"In fact, the other day I ordered a new monitor, and they told me it would take a week to arrive, and it showed up two days later. They established my expectation and then beat it. I was very pleasantly surprised," Carolyn added.

"These folks all seem pretty good at adding feedback and communicating their unique value," Peters said. "Let me look at that list," he told Tom, taking the list and quickly scanning it for other examples. After a few seconds of review, he said, "I think I've seen enough. You folks have been at this a while. Good job. Let's meet again in the morning and talk about how we're going to communicate *our* unique benefit: our ability to deliver within a narrow window of time on an ongoing basis."

Victory

Chapter 19

"We have to provide our customers with feedback," Peters said, kicking off the morning meeting. The overall mood was excellent. Despite the issue with MacroZip that still lingered over the team, there was a growing sense of accomplishment. A deeper understanding of their business had surfaced, and with it an ability to protect the company against an invisible threat: the paradox of excellence.

"How do we make our great service more visible to our customers? How do we reinforce our value?" he continued. "Let's start with what information we already provide to our customers."

"We tell them the number of shipments, the number of boxes, the weight, and the destination," Anne said.

"What else?"

"We have a loss/damage report customers can fill out if there are issues," Carolyn said. "We don't have many problems, so we don't really track it over time, but it does exist."

"We also have a basic cost-per-shipment analysis we provide for our customers. Mostly it just shows up in their monthly report," Tom said.

Peters quickly jotted their ideas on the flipchart. "Okay. That's where we are so far. So do any of these pieces of data reinforce our ability to ship within a narrow window?"

There was silence as the team mulled over the list.

Peters interrupted the silence. "Enough said."

"Can we break out our delivery by the level of time specificity our customers require?" Tom asked.

"It would take a little time," Anne said, since she was responsible for all IT at Premiere. "But it's possible."

"Excellent idea, Tom. How would that work?"

"We'd break down their report by the level of service they required and our performance. If we show we provided the same level of service across different service levels, I think that would be fantastic from a sales perspective."

"Okay, that sounds good. What else could we do?" Peters asked.

"If customers want feedback, we could provide some visibility to where their shipment is at any time. We have the data from each truck. We know exactly where every truck is at any time. For example, once we knew the goods were on the truck in San Diego, we could have found their product much faster than we did and avoided this problem altogether," Carolyn said.

"How would we implement that?" Peters asked. "Technically speaking."

"We'd need to integrate our truck management software and our website together." Tom said.

"It's possible, but it will take some time," Anne said.

"What else?" Peters asked.

"I think we need to sit down with our customers and be more specific about their requirements and our requirements—reinforcing the idea that we're partners," Tom said.

"I've been thinking the same thing after my calls yesterday," Peters added. "What else?"

"We've been working on an update to our website and our marketing collateral. We can focus our message on our outstanding on-time delivery performance versus the industry as a whole. I'm sure I can get permission from the trade association to use that industry data we found the other day," Tom offered.

"We probably need to adjust the monthly reports so we highlight our performance in comparison to competition more effectively," Anne added. "If we change the reporting system, it's conceivable we could integrate it into the accounting system."

Peters laughed. "Anne, I know, 'but it will take some time.'"

They all laughed. The team was finally starting to gel. They were working together and focusing on a common goal: eradicating the paradox of excellence. No longer were they going to lose the chance to highlight Premiere's competitive distinction.

Peters was amazed at how a seemingly catastrophic problem, the potential loss of their largest client, could be so fruitful to the overall health of their business. If anything good had come out of this terrible mess with MacroZip, it had forced Premiere to address a substantial business problem.

Chapter 20

Tuesday morning was glorious and sunny as Tom Fredericks and Hank Peters drove into the MacroZip Electronics parking lot. It was a good omen. They waved to one of their Premiere Specialty Trucking drivers as he exited the facility. *At least MacroZip's still a client for now,* Tom thought. He didn't know what to expect in today's meeting but was confident in Premiere, especially after having the hard evidence in his hands. However, experience had taught him never to take any sales situation for granted. This could be a very tough discussion.

They were eventually led to the corporate boardroom. Sitting behind the broad mahogany table were Frank Sommers, MacroZip Electronics' COO, and Gary Howard, VP of logistics.

Hank Peters took the lead. "Gentlemen, I first want to thank you for giving me some time to get my team together, to understand the situation, and be ready to talk intelligently about it. I appreciate the extra time. Second, I want to apologize for the poor service we gave your firm. I'm sorry for any consequences we've caused in your business. Before going on, I wanted to ask if there's been any warming of relations between MacroZip and Single."

"I think we'll survive the slip-up. They finally acknowledged they made mistakes as well. So we all share some blame," Sommers said, throwing Premiere a small bone.

"Fair enough. If I can be of any assistance in mending the relationship, please let me know," Peters said earnestly. "What I'd like to do now is have our VP of sales and marketing, Tom Fredericks, present our research findings and how we intend to improve our performance over time."

For the next forty-five minutes, Tom walked the two executives through the materials created by Premiere's management team. The team had created an analysis of MacroZip's delivery requirements over time, showing how Premiere continued to deliver higher and higher levels of service without any increases in price. In addition, Carolyn Arnold had found the original contract that had outlined the performance MacroZip had originally desired. Tom was able to highlight how much better Premiere's service was compared to MacroZip's previous trucking service. Gary Howard had not worked at MacroZip at that time, but Frank Sommers remembered the old days. Seeing the actual current performance in comparison to the historic performance was illuminating. MacroZip could also see how Premiere eliminated the problems other shippers caused.

They worked through a planning exercise and established the need for quarterly business reviews to collectively decide how to improve the service and work together as partners. It was a very collaborative effort.

"How did we get into this situation between our companies, Hank?" Sommers asked once the presentation had concluded. "We shouldn't even be having this discussion, should we? What went wrong?"

"Frank, again, let me apologize. This mistake doesn't represent our overall performance. I've learned some things over the past few weeks. I'll tell you this. We're still the best shipping company in Silicon Valley. The facts demonstrate it. I know we'll still have problems on occasion, but I want to assure you personally that we will continue to work hard to eliminate service failure in the future. That said, the reason we're here is we, at Premiere, didn't do a good enough job communicating the value you're getting from us. We overlooked the need to keep you apprised of our service successes and breakdowns." *It won't happen again,* Peters thought to himself.

"Hank, I think we've learned a lot today, too. I trust your team will continue to work as effectively as you have in the past."

"Don't worry, Frank. We will always strive to provide the highest level of quality, period. That said, I'd like you to reconsider and continue with us—at our current rates."

Sommers knew from the presentation the price they were paying was entirely fair, given the true value Premiere was providing. "If you continue your high level of performance, I think we can live with the current price."

"I'm confident in our team. We'll keep our performance up. That's my commitment to you," Peters said. And now he was confident that Premiere's terrific performance would be always visible to every customer, thanks to his discovery of the paradox of excellence.

Peters stood up to shake Frank Sommers' hand. "Let's leave these two to work out the details," Peters said. "You and I have to coordinate our schedules. I need to take you golfing. There's a couple I want you to meet."

Epilogue

Within several months of the meeting with MacroZip, Anne's IT team had redesigned the client reports to highlight Premiere's performance for every client. The Sales Department was thrilled. The clients were thrilled. No one could believe the level of service Premiere had been providing. It was truly outstanding.

Tom Fredericks was having his best year financially. He found it easier to maintain excellent relations with customers because everyone knew what level of service they were receiving. When difficulties arose— which they did—it was easier to appease the client's frustration. So far, the system was working. Tom hadn't lost a single client—not even MacroZip. Not only had MacroZip stayed with Premiere, but had also increased the business the two companies did together.

After golf with Peters and the Jensens, Frank Sommers began successfully using his understanding of the paradox of excellence inside his own organization and was now better managing the relationship between MacroZip and its customers, like Single.

Hank Peters had weighed the options of selling to outsiders versus a management buy-out and had selected the latter. Nine months after the incident with MacroZip, he retired, handing the reigns over to Carolyn Arnold. His golf game was never better.

Carolyn had grown tremendously in the role of CEO. She understood the importance of operational performance, as operational excellence was still the cornerstone of Premiere's competitive differentiation. She had also learned the importance of managing clients' perceptions about that performance. She began relying on Tom Fredericks even more to manage the context by which Premiere was being judged.

By the end of the first year, Tom had instituted an annual survey of customer expectations and satisfaction and found satisfaction with Premiere at an all-time high. Premiere was successfully managing clients' views about the company and its performance. Premiere had found the secret to sustained value by prevailing over their paradox of excellence.

The Interviews

The following is a series of fictional interviews with the key personnel involved in the paradox of excellence story. These interviews occurred three years after the story took place. (You know these people are fictitious, right? Well, then, these interviews are, too!)

Tom Fredericks, VP of Sales and Marketing, Premiere Specialty Trucking

Michael Weissman (MW): Why did MacroZip Electronics' intent to terminate come as such a surprise?

Tom Fredericks (TF): When I was at Jumbo Logistics, MacroZip Electronics kept telling us to measure up to the performance of Premiere. So when I joined Premiere, I had every reason to expect the relationship between Premiere and MacroZip was rock solid. There was no hint of a problem.

MW: How have you kept from being blindsided again?

TF: I've gotten a lot smarter about this. It dawned on me one day that we can never predict the tipping point when we've become invisible and ripe for a crisis. However, I have found a way to identify signs of an emerging problem.

MW: How?

TF: We start by tracking expectations. Have customer expectations changed over the last twelve months? In what ways? We capture expectation information first before we track our own performance. This allows us to assess the criteria by which we are being judged.

MW: What else?

TF: We've built a strategic plan that includes the perceptions we want clients to have about Premiere. The plan deals with issues such as how we want our clients to think about us. What expectations do we want them to have? How do we want them to behave? The plan helps us to shape the way we want our clients to view us. We measure whether our clients value the result we've produced within the context we've established.

MW: Can you give me a practical example of that?

TF: Sure. At Premiere, we decided that our ability to deliver within a narrow window of time was a key benefit. So we set up an annual survey to determine what customers expected in terms of delivery. We knew we could deliver within a two- to three-hour window. We communicated this benefit to our clients and sure enough, the expectations began to climb. Initially, three hours was completely acceptable. Then, over time, our survey showed that clients wanted a two-hour window. Unfortunately, this was impractical. There were too many variables in terms of traffic, loading times, and so on to ensure delivery in that narrow time frame. We had to manage down the customers' expectations. We hired opinion leaders to teach the market that that two-hour delivery was very expensive, unreasonable, and unnecessary. We also showed customers that we were still delivering one hour faster than our competition. This worked. In our most recent survey, the number of people expecting two-hour delivery had declined.

MW: What advice would you have for other people who are reading about the paradox of excellence.

TF: It's easy to blame marketing or sales—to place the responsibility solely on one functional area. But that would be a mistake. Everyone needs to get involved in solving the paradox of excellence because the changes that are needed encompass the entire organization. Let's take us for an example. At Premiere, in order to show our ability to deliver within a narrow window of time, we had to change the reporting system that operations produced. We had to change the reports we received from the information technology group. It caused changes in how we marketed our product and definitely impacted how we sold.

MW: In what way did it impact your sales process?

TF: Before, our selling process was more social—it depended on how well you got along with your client, your schmoozing skills. Now, it is more results focused. We have monthly statements highlighting our performance. In addition, we meet quarterly with each client to compare expected performance with actual performance. We have a lot more data to manage, and this is a challenge. It's changed the character of my job a bit. But having this data in the hands of our reps has provided a forum for frank discussions with our customers and allows our sales reps to be better equipped at managing the customers' expectations.

Carolyn Arnold, CEO of Premiere Specialty Trucking

Dave Mosby (DM): Wow, CEO. Congratulations. The brass ring.

Carolyn Arnold (CA): Ha! It's more like fool's gold [laughs]. Hank Peters is laughing all the way to the bank. I'm still paying for the buy-out, working my butt off while he's out playing golf [laughs again].

DM: How has encountering the paradox of excellence changed your perception of how to run a company?

CA: It changed my perception a lot, actually. I used to think of the organizational parts as clear and distinct: the group that makes the product, the group that sells it, and the group that keeps track of the money. Now, I see it much differently. The paradox of excellence forced me to think of our company as a cohesive unit.

DM: Talk more about that.

CA: You can't fix the paradox of excellence in one area. You can't say that it's a marketing problem, it's more than that. You can't say it's an IT problem—you know, a reporting problem—because it's much more than that. You can't say it's an operations problem, it's much more than that, too. What you come to realize is it's everyone's problem, and everyone needs to work together. The entire customer experience needs to be integrated from operations to marketing and to accounting. You can't guide the overall customer context without seeing the overall customer context your organization is creating. Does that make sense?

DM: Sure does. What one piece of advice would you offer CEOs of service firms?

CA: Teamwork. The paradox of excellence requires teamwork, not fiefdoms. This was the tough lesson I had to learn. It's easy to get lost in the politics of the moment. For a VP striving for a CEO's job, turf matters. Yet my fellow CEOs know, from this vantage point, integration and teamwork are critical. We all have different agendas, and we are always struggling to acquire as much of the scarce resources as possible. However, we can't lose sight that overcoming the paradox of excellence requires that we work together as a team.

DM: Anything else?

CA: Yeah, one more thing. Our motto used to be "Excellence Delivers Victory." Now, because of the paradox of excellence, our new motto is "Excellence *Valued by Customers* Delivers Victory!"

Anne Simpson, CFO Premiere Specialty Trucking

Michael Weissman (MW): Anne, tell our readers how the paradox of excellence circumstance affected you.

Anne Simpson (AS): It was a nightmare. It generated lots of new crises for me to handle. As head of the computer team, we had to make enormous changes to our programs and our reports. It was an exhausting time for my team. Everyone saw how Premiere was being taken for granted by MacroZip, but no one saw how my group was being taken for granted by our own management team.

MW: Didn't you get any accolades for all your hard work?

AS: No! [laughs] It's another example of the paradox of excellence, I know. It's funny, but so true. The paradox of excellence doesn't only apply to companies. We're an internal service department. We supply accounting services, human resource services, and IT services to our internal customers. They treat us the same way MacroZip treated Premiere. We work hard to get a particularly difficult piece of computer code written, and it's no big deal. Our great performance is ignored, overlooked. It can be very frustrating.

MW: Have you found it difficult to manage expectations inside the organization?

AS: Yes, it's been extraordinarily difficult—probably much harder than it was dealing with MacroZip.

MW: Why do you say that?

AS: MacroZip is a paying customer—a big paying customer. When you're about to lose millions of dollars in revenues, you make it happen—whatever "it" is. In that kind of crisis, cost really doesn't matter. However, an internal client might be important, but they're not as important as an external customer.

Therefore there are far fewer resources available to establish benchmarks and other ways to reinforce your value. It's far more difficult.

MW: Have you found a solution?

AS: I know you're looking for an easy answer. Unfortunately, I don't have one for you. Sorry. It's really hard. If you try to manage expectations too much, you are viewed as a "sandbagger," and people continue to have unrealistically high expectations. If you try to be a voice of reason—a common issue when dealing with technical matters—and show the risks to the schedule, you can be viewed as an impediment to the schedule, not a voice of reason. I'd love a solution. If you have one, let me know.

MW: One thing to think about is your value. Let's take computers for an example. You say that you're getting "pushback" when you provide realistic milestones for your schedules. Is that right?

AS: Yeah, that's right.

MW: Well, the problem that I see is a difference of people's points of view. You think managing time-lines—knowing what it takes to get a job done right—is critical. Would you agree?

AS: Yes.

MW: Therefore, you have decided that is where you add value. True?

AS: I'd agree. That's a fair statement.

MW: Well, it appears to me that your internal clients have a different point of view. They don't see the value of your reasoned expertise. Therefore, if you want to manage the context in which you're judged, you need to elevate the importance of managing schedules in their overall priority. They need to agree with you on what's important. Once you do that, you will be much more likely to be viewed as valuable and wise in the eyes of your internal customers.

AS: Thanks. That's good advice. I need to think about how I add value in each of my different areas of responsibility.

MW: What else have you learned from this experience with the paradox of excellence?

AS: As you know, I am responsible for human resources. For the last five years, we have been performing 360-degree reviews. Do you know what those are?

MW: Yes. Those are the reviews where your subordinates, your peers, and your superior evaluate your performance. How does that relate to the paradox?

AS: We use a standardized performance appraisal system to obtain opinions of job performance across each of these constituents. Yet we never get the expectation behind the opinion. Remember, a perception of performance is a comparison of performance against some expectation. We were getting the perception of performance without a clear under-standing of the expectation. Sure these performance appraisals provide some standardized, objective crite-ria. However, these appraisals don't ever capture the continuously rising expectations the employee receives each year. For example, a truck driver who's been with our company for ten years will have higher performance expectations placed on him than a driver who's only been here two years. It's just human nature, and it's not captured in our 360-degree review system.

MW: What are you doing about it?

AS: We've put a team together with people from each part of the organization to review how to change our review system. We don't want to abandon the practice of 360-degree reviews. We still believe they're a good idea. However, we hope in the next three to six months to roll out a new approach, one where expectations are built into the review.

MW: Any words of wisdom to our readers about the paradox of excellence concept?

AS: I hadn't thought about it this way until our discussion right now, but if you're an employee, the paradox applies to you as well. You need to know how to communicate your true value every day. In addition, if you are a service provider within an organization—be it operations, facilities, HR, accounting, purchasing, marketing, you name it, I don't care what you do—just remember to reinforce your value all the time. Be sensitive to the way you do it. Don't be obnoxious or obvious. That won't help you at all. Yet don't shy away from your need to manage people's expectations every day. That's my advice.

Hank Peters, Founder and Retired CEO of Premiere Specialty Trucking

Dave Mosby (DM): Tell me about your encounter with the paradox of excellence.

Hank Peters (HP): It was like running into a brick wall. The shock from the paradox of excellence experience has changed my life in so many ways. Of course, it was very helpful in sustaining my business at a critical time. My business would have faded away without any hope of recovery, and I would never have known why. But I think the paradox of excellence has changed my *personal* life more than my professional life.

DM: Really? That's a surprise. Tell me more about what you mean.

HP: The paradox of excellence has taught me a lot about being more in tune with expectation management than I ever was before. It's kept me focused on what people expect from me, what they see as valuable. It's hard for a Marine like me to be sensitive to other people's expectations. I've lived my life more concerned with *my* goals and *my* behavior. If you do the right thing and live by the ideal that "Excellence Delivers Victory," you succeed. These self-focused mottos have been central to my thinking for years. Now that I've retired, personal relationships, not professional relationships, are more critical. I'm a grandfather now. I want to be a positive influence in my grandkids' lives. That's my new agenda. Kids these days have so many expectations. They feel they are entitled to everything. I want to balance what they want from me and what I think is best. If I want to be valued by my grandkids, I have to manage how they perceive me. Otherwise, they won't listen to what I have to say. It's a delicate balance.

DM: That's great! The paradox is found in all kinds of relationships, not just relationships between a buyer and seller. What advice would you give people about preparing for the paradox of excellence?

HP: First, be vigilant, because the paradox of excellence is like a land mine. It's hard to see, but it's real, and it can show up anywhere, anytime. Also, don't lose the big picture. Many people can misconstrue the lesson here. The paradox of excellence is not about style over substance. It's not about creating false perceptions or creating a mirage. Don't believe that creating some artificial image is the same as managing expectations. It's not. It's about understanding your real value and reinforcing it. You still have to perform well. It's about managing the context, the criteria. It's about leading your industry, not following it. Look, be great at what you do in life, be it personally or professionally. Be authentic and true to who you really are. Be self-assured, yet don't overcommit, don't overpromise. Keep expectations reasonable. Everyone will be much happier in life. Take it from an old Marine, "Semper Fi!"

Ryan Walters, VP of Sales at NEWCO Logistics and Former Sales Representative for Premiere Specialty Trucking

Michael Weissman (MW): Tell me what's been going on with you. I heard you left Premiere.

Ryan Walters (RW): That's right. I left there over a year ago. It was a chance for me to finally become a VP of sales myself.

MW: Congratulations. What did you learn from the paradox of excellence while you were at Premiere?

RW: I've learned more about the paradox here at my new job than I did at Premiere.

MW: How so?

RW: Premiere was a great, well-run company. The operational performance was very high. The paradox of excellence was a critical but manageable issue. However, at my new company, it's really different.

Our performance hasn't been so stellar. When I first got here, I didn't think the paradox of excellence even applied to us. Nobody thinks about a paradox of mediocrity! Boy, was I wrong!

MW: Why do you say that?

RW: When I got here, our reputation was in the tank. Nobody was happy with our performance. Everybody expected us to make mistakes, miss shipments, mess up deliveries—you name it. I was part of the turnaround team—the team brought in to fix the company's problems. We embarked on a continuous performance improvement plan. We began fixing our performance, but we weren't gaining any stature in the industry. I was confused. In retrospect, I should have known better, having gone through the same issue at Premiere. But I have to admit that I didn't see it at first. The paradox of excellence applies to every company in every phase of its corporate life. In fact, our situation here is probably more common than what we saw at Premiere. At NEWCO, we had bad performance, but a worse reputation. Therefore, our performance exceeded customers' expectations. However, as we improved, the expectations began to grow, eventually outstripping our ability to improve. Customers were becoming hopeful and optimistic—obviously something a sales VP wants in a client base. Yet it created the paradox of excellence all over again!

MW: What a great story. What advice would you have for readers who are learning about the paradox of excellence for the first time?

RW: Don't be in denial. Take a good hard look at your organization. Look at your marketing communication: How bombastic are you? How much hype is there? Are your sales reps overselling the performance? If they are, you're in for serious trouble. But let's say your organization isn't overselling. Take a deep look and see what your customers expect. When your operations or service delivery team does an excellent job, does the customer cheer, or is the customer indifferent to your performance? If the customer is indifferent, that's a telltale sign you are having a problem.

161

Sam Clark, Certified Financial Planner

David Mosby (DM): Sam, thanks for taking the time to talk with us about the paradox of excellence. How has this idea changed how you run your own business?

Sam Clark (SC): It's a pleasure to talk with you, Dave. My business is a little different than Premiere's business. They provide a clear service: moving products from point A to point B. Financial planning is different; our service is less tangible. When Hank and I began talking about this paradox of excellence, the idea had as much impact on my business as it did on his. I started to think about the value I provide and how I reinforce it. It caused me to reevaluate how I handled my accounts.

DM: Be specific. In what ways did your account management change?

SC: Previously, I saw account management as all about interpersonal relationships. People bought from me because of my personality. There's nothing wrong with that approach. It has stood by me for decades. Yet as I started to think about the paradox of excellence, I realized that was not my differentiator. It was not reinforcing my core value. When I stopped to think about it, my job has always been to make my clients the most amount of money for the amount of risk they're willing to assume. My knowledge of each client's special needs is what sets me apart—my value-add.

DM: Wasn't that always the case?

SC: Sure, but I always used personal relationships as my primary marketing weapon. I thought the unique value was not my wisdom; it was me, Sam, my personality. But there was a problem. Many in my elderly client base were dying. It was then when I realized my existing strategy wasn't working. My relationship had always been with the primary financial person in the household. When the financial matters were transferred over to the next of kin, many of these new clients started to look solely at the performance of the portfolio and never considered the personal relationship. I started to lose accounts. My relationship was with the deceased, not with the new person responsible for finances. Then it hit me: I hadn't been reinforcing my value along the way—you know, in the reports and financial returns. I would run the typical reports of each client's net worth and compare it to the stock market or some standardized index. Yet that's not how I actually invested. I always thought about the risk each client was willing to take and optimized their return based upon their risk profile.

DM: That's fascinating. What did you begin to do differently?

SC: I started to build comparisons of performance based upon investments of equal risk. What I found thrilled me. While I always knew in my heart that I was doing a good job, I never had the kind of validation that came from doing this type of comparison. I had performed far better than these comparative investments. When I started sharing that information with my clients, my value became clearer. It also made it easier to communicate my value to other people within the family when the unfortunate time arose to move the account to a new person.

DM: What advice do you have for people regarding the paradox of excellence?

SC: Don't wait until you have a crisis. Don't wait until it's too late. Why go through the hardship I went through or Hank went through? Be smart and proactive. Start thinking about how you can modify your operations right now. Today. What can you do differently? Don't delay—that would be my message. Don't delay.

PART TWO: The Models

The Concept

The Assessment

The Roadmap for Success

The Concept

Overview of the Paradox of Excellence

The Paradox of Excellence

The better you do your job, the more invisible you become—to everything but bad news. At the same time, your perceived value erodes as customers lose sight of the problems you relieve.

Symptoms

- Small problems become big problems.
- You feel underappreciated or undervalued.
- Customers are switching from you for no apparent reason.
- Customers focus on minor attributes more than main features.
- Customers are more price sensitive without reason.

Root Cause

You neglect to reinforce your distinguishing value, leaving customers to evaluate your performance in the heat of the moment.

Root Behaviors and Assumptions

- You spend more time communicating with prospects than with long-term customers.
- You assume that customers will observe performance improvements and value them.
- You assume customers will put those improvements in context of the entire market and the competition.
- You forget that customers need this context to evaluate your performance.
- You force customers to set their own context and let them use their own criteria.

The Remedy

Provide timely and socially acceptable reinforcement of the distinguishing value you deliver to your customers.

The Assessment

The Assessment

A re you suffering from the paradox of excellence? Do you know whether the ideas presented in this book apply to you? There is one sure-fire way to find out: take this brief self-assessment.

The following twenty questions will help you determine whether you are suffering from the paradox.

Each "yes" is worth one point. "No" is worth 0 points. A score over 15 means you are highly at risk or already suffering from the paradox. A score between 10–15 means you are moderately at risk. As you'd expect, companies with scores below 10 are less likely to be suffering from the paradox.

Self-Assessment

Are any of the following circumstances true today?	YES 1 point	NO 0 points
1 Your company is usually the sole supplier of your class of product or service to your customer.	☐	☐
2 Customers have grown to consider your company's performance as highly reliable.	☐	☐
3 Your company's performance is the industry benchmark and/or is used to judge the performance of competitors.	☐	☐
4 It's been a long time since your company has had a "performance" problem.	☐	☐
5 Customers are indifferent and seem not to care what your company does.	☐	☐
6 Your company's performance, especially its special efforts, is often invisible to customers.	☐	☐

	YES 1 point	NO 0 points
7 You feel your company's performance is underappreciated and taken for granted by customers.	☐	☐
8 Customers have difficulty distinguishing your company's performance from that of your competitors.	☐	☐
9 Your company is experiencing arbitrary pressure to lower prices.	☐	☐
10 Customers have difficulty quantifying your company's positive impact on their business.	☐	☐
11 Customers appear more focused on secondary attributes of your service than on your primary attributes.	☐	☐
12 Customers have difficulty articulating your company's distinguishing value from that of others.	☐	☐

Have any of the following circumstances happened in the last year?	YES 1 point	NO 0 points
13 An existing customer opened your company's service contract to competitive bid for the first time.	☐	☐
14 A customer states that the service your company provides is a commodity.	☐	☐
15 A customer suddenly terminates (or threatens to terminate) your company's service or relationship.	☐	☐
16 Customers are not advocating your company to others as favorably or frequently as before.	☐	☐
17 Your company's margins have declined.	☐	☐
18 Customers were too happy or too upset over a trivial performance matter.	☐	☐

	YES 1 point	**NO** 0 points
19 Customer feedback was conflicting (both positive and negative) regarding the same performance.	☐	☐
20 Customer expectations became increasingly unrealistic.	☐	☐

The Roadmap for Success

The Remedy

The remedy for overcoming the paradox of excellence is to continuously reinforce your distinguishing value in a socially acceptable manner. The Continuous Visibility Wheel, shown on the next page, will help you discover your distinguishing value and develop socially acceptable ways to reinforce that value.

1. Discover the Expectations

To address the paradox of excellence, you must first identify the existing expectations prospects and customers use to evaluate your performance and discover how those expectations are impacting your business.

The Goals for This Phase
To develop a comprehensive list of attributes the market uses to evaluate your performance, to clarify existing expectations for each attribute, and to know how the market perceives your and your competition's performance on those attributes.

The Continuous Visibility Wheel

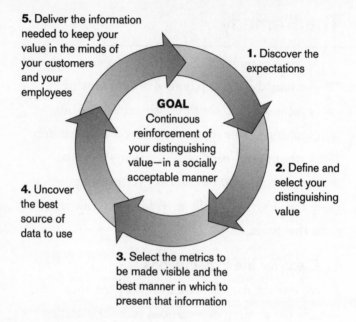

5. Deliver the information needed to keep your value in the minds of your customers and your employees

1. Discover the expectations

GOAL
Continuous reinforcement of your distinguishing value—in a socially acceptable manner

2. Define and select your distinguishing value

4. Uncover the best source of data to use

3. Select the metrics to be made visible and the best manner in which to present that information

Our Recommended Approach

1. Develop a list of attributes prospects and customers use to evaluate your organization, your products or services, and your competition.

   a. Leverage internal resources by interviewing frontline workers, reviewing internal marketing materials and customer complaint data, and meeting with internal product and service developers to discover what they believe are the important attributes.

b. Review external secondary research sources such as trade articles about customer needs and vendor performance, websites discussing customer issues, competitive marketing materials, and available third-party market research data.

c. Perform in-depth interviews with prospects and customers to discover unspoken expectations and attributes they use when assessing performance.

d. Produce a comprehensive list of attributes, the criteria customers use to assess your performance, and the possible measurement criteria used to render that assessment when evaluating your performance (the expectation).

2. Track and prioritize these attributes, the market's expectations, and satisfaction of your performance over time using existing or new data collection.

3. Determine the customer context you will manage going forward by capturing unrealistic expectations, discovering the reasons for those expectations (your performance, market trends,

competitive positioning, or other factors), and estimating the impact of better managing those expectations.

4. Identify existing customers who are at risk of abandoning their relationship with your firm due to unmet expectations and begin to reestablish realistic expectations on an ad-hoc basis.

Tips on Improving the Process

- When reviewing what customers really value, be open to the surprising attributes they hold as valuable.
- Check for what triggers "crisis relationships."
- Assess whether the market is ignoring performance you believe is important.
- Discover which ways your value might be eroding.

Common Mistakes to Avoid

- Don't just use product or service attributes when developing a list of what matters to customers. Be willing to consider company attributes, even attributes related to your overall ecosystem (such as channel partners).

- Don't limit the attributes to primary features. Often secondary features become more important over time.
- Avoid suggestive discussions when talking with customers. Don't direct the conversation; let the customer control what gets covered.
- Resist excusing away problems uncovered during the assessment.

2. Define and Select Your Distinguishing Value

Distinguishing value is a relevant promise only you can offer to a prospect or customer. The promise is based upon the customer's perspective, not yours. Moreover, the promise must be credible. Customers must be able to believe your organization could deliver such value. In addition, this value should be defensible over time. Finally, your distinguishing value should inoculate your firm from becoming invisible and from temporary dips in performance.

The Goal for This Phase
To create a succinct, believable statement of the sustainable distinguishing value you will make visible.

Our Recommended Approach

There are five main steps in discovering and defining your value:

1. Measure your company's performance against key competitors to uncover opportunities and threats.

   a. Review perceived performance for each company from the tracking studies.

   b. Review expectations in performance for each company.

   c. Assess the gap between perceived and expected performance for each company.

2. Build a strategy for dealing with the gaps. Here are some strategic alternatives:

   a. Emphasize high performance where expectations are being met, but your overall performance is higher than your competitors.

   b. Emphasize where performance equals the market, but customer expectations are unrealistic. This will help recalibrate expectations.

   c. Emphasize the long term, where performance is excellent—but cannot be sustained. When a problem does emerge, customers will see it as an anomaly.

d. When leadership is difficult, shift the customer's expectation to your level of performance, rendering the competitor's advantage as superfluous. Concurrently, develop a new area of value, promote its importance, and demonstrate your performance within that new area.

3. Prioritize the choices and select the value that best inoculates your company from becoming invisible or losing value when a temporary dip in performance occurs.

4. Consider which area you can own over the long term.

5. Focus on delivering excellent performance in this area of advantage. Build goals for individuals, departments, and the entire company around this area of distinction.

Tips on Improving the Process
Several questions are useful in deciding what to make visible:

- Which part of your value-add is easiest to expose?
- In which area of value do you have the most consistently positive performance?
- Which attributes are defensible over the long term?
- How might communicating this value alter customer expectations?
- How can this information help manage the context by which you are being evaluated?

Common Mistakes to Avoid

- Don't start with too many potential areas to make visible. Start with fewer than five.
- Recognize that importance doesn't equal relevance. If everyone offers the same performance, that performance becomes irrelevant in the buying decision.
- Avoid areas that are easy for a competitor to emulate. Pick an area in which you can hold the distinctive edge for a long time.
- Don't move to the next phase until you can describe your distinguishing value in less than

thirty seconds and fifteen words. However, don't confuse brevity and clarity with perfection. Striving for perfection is a big trap to avoid.

• Don't lose sight of the context by which you are being assessed and value is bestowed.

3. Select the Metrics to Be Made Visible and the Best Manner in Which to Present That Information

There are many potential ways to share information that reinforces your distinguishing value including: report cards, scheduled status meetings, smiles by service providers, regular access to top executives, in monthly invoices, or in advertisements. One of the greatest opportunities for innovation is in the manner by which you make your value visible. Take time to explore different potential approaches.

The Goal for This Phase

A clear statement of the performance metrics you will publish and the method of presentation you will use to best reinforce your value.

Our Recommended Approach

1. Choose the unit of measurement that will best demonstrate your performance.
2. Select a socially acceptable method of communicating that value.
   a. Study how your prospects and customers behave before and after they buy your product or service.
   b. Identify how buyers use information to make decisions (individually or collectively).
   c. Determine the learning style of your audience to ensure that your information is appropriately framed. (For example, do they prefer concrete or abstract information?)
   d. Consider the frequency of communication as well as the method.
3. Decide the best way to present the metrics.
   a. Choose the context within which your data will be presented.
      i. Isolated: your performance by itself

  ii. Comparative:

   1. Your performance versus competitors

   2. Your performance versus industry norms/benchmarks

   3. Your current performance versus previous performance

 b. Select a suitable presentation method

  i. Visual (charts, graphs, tables, video)

  ii. Narrative (stories, descriptions)

  iii. Spoken (interpersonal interaction)

  iv. Combination of the above

Tips on Improving the Process

- Focus on the results produced rather than the actions performed.
- The better you understand your customer's behavior, the faster the process will go. Invest more time up front to save time later on.
- Don't prioritize during brainstorming sessions. Wait until all the new ideas are communicated before editing and prioritizing the list.

- Consider the following ways to potentially reinforce your value:
  1. Volume: How much are you doing for the customer?
  2. Velocity: How fast are you doing it?
  3. Quality: How well are you doing it? (Against service level agreements, for example.)
  4. Cost: How much are you charging the customer to do it?

Common Mistakes to Avoid

- Don't limit yourself to the existing data you currently collect. Often, the value your organization will expose is not revealed in existing reports.
- Don't assume that more communication is better than less. Understand the social norms in your market before presuming more is better.
- Avoid the tendency to overcomplicate the requirement. Keep it simple and clear. In many cases, a single data point is just as relevant as a complex chart.
- Avoid self-promotion. The paradox of excellence is not about tooting your own horn; it is about honest communication of real performance and

receiving appropriate value for that performance. Self-promotion doesn't fix the paradox of excellence; it only exacerbates it.

4. Uncover the Best Source of Data to Use

Find or develop the information system that supplies that data.

The Goal for This Phase

Identify and select existing sources of data or develop a plan for systematically acquiring the required information.

Our Recommended Approach

1. Review existing reports to see if the data are readily available from a single source.
2. If not, determine if multiple sources of existing data can be integrated to deliver the desired information.
3. Be willing to develop new ways to generate, capture, integrate, and/or present data about your company's distinguishing value.
   a. Determine the needed changes to the existing systems and organization.

b. Establish a detailed plan with timing and budgets needed to make these changes possible.

Tips on Improving the Process
Have a clear idea of what you're looking for. Be sure to work from a specification. (If you don't, revisit Step Three.)

Common Mistakes to Avoid
- Stay focused on the information you wish to share, not the information you have available to share.
- Don't make the remedy fit the existing data—it will only weaken the remedy.
- Don't confuse "interesting" with useful.
- Resist the temptation to "fiddle" with the numbers to make your performance look better. The more authentic the information you present, the stronger the brand loyalty you build.

5. Deliver the Information Needed to Keep Your Value in the Minds of Your Customers and Your Employees

Step Five is all about making your value visible.

The Goals for This Phase

To develop a specific, repeatable business process to reinforce continuously your distinguishing value and to develop the organization, infrastructure, and systems to support that process economically.

Our Recommended Approach

1. Have executives kick off the program to stress the importance of the remedy to employees and to make the initiative tangible.
2. Set clear goals and timelines.
3. Allocate the appropriate resources to implement the changes you have specified.
4. Build and implement the new systems and organizational processes.
5. Train the team on how to benefit from the new systems.

Tips on Improving the Process

- Help employees get aligned with your plan and keep them informed of the intent, status, and results of your efforts.

- Create an environment where employees can safely present truthful information about existing systems or performance.

Common Mistakes to Avoid

- Don't try to do everything at once. Use a phased approach. Pick the area of greatest leverage as a starting point and work from there.
- Don't try to automate everything.
- Don't limit the paradox of excellence remedy to marketing and/or sales functions. This only limits possible solutions and reduces the likelihood a remedy will be adopted companywide.
- Don't wait too long before telling employees about the process you are deploying. Keep them well informed about the purpose, process, and status of your efforts.

Acknowledgments

Writing is a lot like popcorn. As a writer, you start with a small, hard kernel of an idea that no one wants. Then you add a little oil and heat up the idea. As you cook, the heat transforms your little idea into something people love: a tasty, tasty piece of popped corn.

In the process of writing this parable, dozens of people were our fire—our catalyst to growth and maturity. We'd like to thank our wives, children, parents, and siblings who shared the burden of continuous revisions and incessant talk about the book.

We especially want to thank Jesus Christ for inspiring us personally and professionally each and every day.

All glory, credit, and thanks belong to Him—the greatest sufferer of the paradox of excellence the world will ever know.

There are many people we need to thank for helping us with the creation of *The Paradox of Excellence.* First, we'd like to thank Tom Niehaus for inspiring us to write an entertaining book, not just an informative one. We also want to thank the many people who helped review the book: Tim Allen, Andres Bergero, Steve Bertges, Craig Bidondo, Layne Bradley, John Brassner, Ilya Brook, Julie Choate, Al Clary, Katherine Conrad, Vicky deYoung, Len DiGiovanni, Jeff Eitzen, Debby Goldberg, Paul Grabowsky, Don and Karen Gray, Tom Greensmith, Harry Hiner, Dave and Patty Jensen, Lauren Johnson, Mike Kelly, Graham Lammers, Mel Lemberger, Greg Livengood, Sharon Lyon, Marc Mandel, Peter Mantas, Frank Martin, Jim McGrail, Jackie Meyer, Michael Murray, Bill Nichols, Ron Okamoto, Judith Parker, Pierce Plam, Dwayne Price, Bill Reimers, Robert Riegel, Karin Runge, Jon Safer, Chris and Charlie Salas, Sam Sawires, Rob Schock, Rajesh

Setty, Randy Sherrod, Clark Smith, Mike Stone, Merwick Tam, Mike Tye, Bob Verret, Dick Ward, Gary Waymire, Paul Witkay, and Joan Wright.

Finally, we'd like to thank our literary agent, Jim Levine, our editor, Susan Williams—whose keen business sense immediately drew us to her and to Jossey-Bass—and all the great people at Jossey-Bass—including Mary Garrett, Carolyn Carlstroem, Rob Brandt, and Karen Warner—for adding the butter and salt—the needed ingredients for our idea to sell, well, like popcorn.

About the Authors

D*avid Mosby* is CEO of InterWorks Software, Inc., a software development firm that creates specialized customer retention and value reinforcement solutions and has built solutions for many companies including DHL, Kaiser Permanente, and Link Logistics/Starbucks.

Dave's thirty-five years of experience in high technology includes nearly twenty years in CEO positions. Prior to starting InterWorks, Dave was president and CEO of Softguard Systems, Inc., a publicly traded software company, where he led the company to a market capitalization growth of 2,500 percent in three years. Prior to that, he was president of The Systems Support Group and led teams at SAGE

Software, Boole & Babbage, and University Computing Company. He started his technology career at the NSA and Strategic Air Command.

Michael Weissman, a leading expert in business growth strategies, is founder and president of Fresh Perspectives, a San Francisco Bay Area consulting firm. Michael has helped companies of all sizes including Adobe Systems, Apple Computer, Fidelity Investments, Hewlett Packard, and Intel find new, practical ways to maximize their sales, profits, and value.

Previously, Michael led marketing at several high technology firms where he generated over $600 million in new business growth and helped these companies win awards for products, promotions, web design, and branding. He holds business degrees from Babson College and the University of California, Irvine.

To learn more about the paradox of excellence, share success stories, provide suggestions, or reach either Dave or Michael, please visit *www.paradoxofexcellence.com*